CELEBRATING FIFTY

CELEBRATING FIFTY

Women Share Their Experiences, Challenges, and Insights on Becoming 50

■

KAREN BLAKER, Ph.D.

CB
CONTEMPORARY
BOOKS
CHICAGO

Library of Congress Cataloging-in-Publication Data

Blaker, Karen.
    Celebrating fifty : women share their experiences, challenges, and insights on becoming 50 / Karen Blaker.
       p.   cm.
    ISBN 0-8092-4262-1 (cloth) : $17.95
    1. Middle aged women—United States.   I. Title.
HQ1059.5.U5B53   1990
305.4—dc20   90-40575
                                                                                                         CIP

What follows are the real-life experiences and thoughts of women who are celebrating or have recently celebrated their fiftieth birthday. To protect the rights of those whom the author interviewed, certain characters' names have been changed, and some of the events have been altered.

Copyright © 1990 by Karen Blaker
All rights reserved
Published by Contemporary Books, Inc.
180 North Michigan Avenue, Chicago, Illinois 60601
Manufactured in the United States of America
International Standard Book Number: 0-8092-4262-1

Dedicated to fifty women who helped make this book possible through their willingness to share the experience of turning fifty:

Naomi E.	Dorothy H.
Joyce F.	Patsy K.
Carol F.	Joan S.
Mary T.	Daphne R.
Marilyn R.	Linda C.
Sylvia McC.	Susan B.
Sharon H.	Diane S.
June P.	Laura L.
Corinne B.	Sue R.
Martha W.	Irene K.
Linda S.	Ruthann S.
Ruth B.	Nessa P.
Dee H.	Dona B.
Katie B.	Pat T.
Judy R.	Ina D.
Diane M.	Nancy J.
Marcy S.	Marcia C.
Rosemary H.	Karen R.
Penny G.	Nancy J.
Sally L.	Joanne H.
Jane D.	Betsy E.
Karen S.	Jean McK.
Susan P.	Nancy F.
Jeannie B.	Barbara S.
Katherine B.	Barbara F.

Contents

Acknowledgments ix
Introduction: This Is What Fifty Looks Like! 1
1 A New Way to Act Our Age 15
2 Affirming the Change of Life 33
3 A Time of Achievement 53
4 Beauty Lost and Found 67
5 Beyond the Mother Role 89
6 Our Parents' Keepers 107
7 In Search of Community 121
8 A Celebration of Fifty 145
  Appendix A: Recommended Reading 163
  Appendix B: Reader Survey: Turning Fifty 167

Acknowledgments

The completion of this book depended on the support of many talented and generous people. In particular I would like to thank Jane Dystel, my literary agent and friend. Jane knows how to recognize a winning book idea, and she knows how to make it happen. She stimulates my thought processes, encourages me during slumps, and always takes good care of me.

This book could not have been written without the help of my collaborator, Catherine Whitney. I am grateful to Catherine for her friendship, her patience, and her unique ability to arrange words on the printed page so they say what I want them to say. She's an effective sounding board for the development of ideas, and she was a great person to have at my side during this project.

Jill Needham, my editor at Contemporary Books, deserves my gratitude for having the courage to believe in a book about women turning fifty and for her skillful editing and valuable input. Nancy Coffey, formerly at Contemporary, has my thanks for putting herself behind this project in its early stages.

I have been richly blessed with two wonderful children, Scott and Kim. I would like to thank them for their support and for knowing how to handle a mother turning fifty. I am also thankful to my parents, Gretchen and Harlan, for all they have given me in fifty years of life. And I am especially thankful to Bob, who has loved me in good times and bad.

Baggywrinkle

Baggywrinkle on a sailboat quiet at anchor
Drops me deep into myself.
I reflect like the water, backwards in time.
Grab the present!
Futurize.

A young girl, twenty-six
made baggywrinkle for some handsome sailors
on a deck somewhere in Spain.
Untwisted the rope, cut with nasty knife.
Tied on, transformed to protect our sails.

The rope tied us to the land,
strong, solid in one powerful line.
Now in small pieces, in twists
a wrinkly, wiry beard around the lines.
Cushioned, safe, sails won't chafe.

Why now at fifty does this image cut so deep?
Is baggywrinkle what I carry
under my upper arms, my chin, my butt?
Has it grown over my sleek lines?
Yes! And I am angry.

I thought my journey would be smooth.
Marriage, family, career.
After each storm I limp into port
baggywrinkled, weathered, tired.
What am I supposed to learn?

Voyage on! is my lesson.
Plenty of incredible adventures ahead.
With a crimson sunset behind me,
earth energy flows in me.
(Or was that a hot flash?)
I breathe into my own sails.

I am at the helm now
Baggywrinkled with wisdom and tears,
Sails sense, stretch and surge forward.
Mighty winds lift my wings
My faith, my loves and my friends.

*by Diane Sanson, fifty, who has
been my friend since the seventh grade
November 1989*

CELEBRATING FIFTY

Introduction
This Is What Fifty Looks Like!

This year I turn fifty, and I find myself awed by the way a full half century has sneaked up and caught me by surprise. I certainly don't *feel* fifty—at least not in the way I always believed that fifty would feel. I have energy. I'm healthy. I have work I love. And I think I look pretty good, too. I feel the way Mary Tyler Moore must have felt when she expressed surprise and exhilaration at reaching the half-century mark. In a May 1988 *Redbook* interview she mused, "When I was 22, I said to myself, 'Mary, someday it's going to be important to be younger than you really are.' So from that moment on, I just kept lying about my age. I lied all my life. Then, last year, when I was about to turn fifty, I couldn't contain myself anymore. I thought it was so fantastic to turn fifty and look as good as I looked, that I was practically stopping strangers on the street to tell them how old I really was."

At first the idea of turning fifty seemed a bit frightening. I found myself peering in the mirror, wondering if people would be able to guess my age by looking at my face (and fearing that they would!). Sometimes I would hide my hands, because they looked old with their blue veins and emerging brown spots. When I came across friends I hadn't seen for a while, I was surprised to notice how obviously they had aged.

I began to mourn in small ways the roads I had not traveled and probably never would. Oddly, I also began to forget my age and stumble a bit when I tried to recall if I was forty-eight or forty-nine. When a minor case of arthritis sent me to the doctor, I was stricken with the thought "I am now getting old people's diseases." It also became harder for me to laugh off simple embarrassments; when my shoulder pads popped out on the volleyball court, I felt my face burn when everyone laughed.

But gradually, as I began to examine my feelings on a deeper level and listen to what other women were saying, I realized that a shift of monumental proportions had taken place in the way women relate to reaching the turning point of fifty. Most of the women who have shared their experiences with me have said that they don't feel in the least bit over-the-hill. Their time lines for aging have changed, even if society at large has not yet adjusted to the change. With life expectancies for healthy American women now averaging more than eighty years, women of fifty refuse to be called old.

Even so, most women share the view that this age represents a time of reckoning, a "now or never" point in their lives. I have felt it too. During the past five years time has grown more precious and I have been less likely to waste it on projects or people I don't like. I have realized that I must take action in pursuit of my dreams or risk having them remain unfulfilled. This urgency is not a desperate feeling born of the fear that time is running out on me. Rather, it is I who am doing the running these days, and I'm enjoying the surprises I find when I turn each corner.

I have enjoyed exploring the roads not taken, even those that branched off in radical directions. One of these roads was fashion modeling. I can't exactly pinpoint the reason that the idea of modeling appealed so much to me. Perhaps it was because I sensed it might be a tremendous affirmation of my femininity at a time when I needed it the most. Or maybe I just liked the idea of so dramatically switching career images—from the mind work of psychotherapy to the body work of modeling. Whatever the reasons, when I turned forty-seven, on a whim I joined a gym, worked out for a few months to get in shape, and had my husband, Bob, take a few pictures of me. These I sent off to an agency that specialized in mature models. I was excited when they accepted me and sent me on a job. I learned that modeling wasn't for me, but it was kind of fun as a one-time experience. And I felt a deep satisfaction that I had pursued an old dream and made it come to life. At an age when women are often made to feel less powerful I felt stronger than ever.

But even as the future beckoned, I was more aware than ever of the embrace of the past. It is common to think a lot about your adolescence as you approach fifty, and it makes sense that this is so. In a way fifty marks the beginning of a second adolescence. The changes in your body are reminiscent of those that occurred in puberty. There is another raging hormonal turmoil that sets you off balance. And, at the same time, there's a similar revived expectation about the future, a rebirth of the freedom to be *you*. It is a better thing, in many ways, this freedom, than the one in your youth that was inspired by rebellion or naïveté. Yet at the time it occurs, it feels like a crisis, and the idea of celebrating this milestone seems anathema to many women.

What's so great about being fifty? I've been asked. On the face of it fifty may seem a regrettable landmark. But there's so much more to it than that. I've reached an awareness in my own life of the possibilities surrounding this threshold. I've seen it in the faces of my contemporaries and heard it in the tales and reflections of hundreds of women across the nation. It is this previously well-kept secret that I am now so anxious to share.

※ ※

The "change of life" took me by surprise, as it does many women, and at first I didn't even notice the signs. After the fact was confirmed by my doctor, I felt strangely excited, and I looked around for someone to tell. This was definitely a rite of passage that needed to be shared. That evening I decided to turn a previously planned dinner out with my twenty-one-year-old daughter into a celebration, just as we had celebrated her rite of passage into the future when she got her first period. I told her my news, and we clinked our glasses together in a toast across the span of a generation.

"You know," I said to her later, "it feels funny to be approaching the time when I won't be able to have children anymore."

"Oh, Mom," she said with a laugh, "what difference does it make? You don't really want more children, do you?"

"No. But the idea of it is something I'll have to get used to. It means I'm moving out of that phase and into the next phase of my life. It will be new—being a caretaker won't be so important in my life anymore. I have to figure out where I'm going to channel those energies. It's a little scary, but I'm excited."

Anthropologist Margaret Mead, a woman ahead of her time, once defined the feelings of anticipation that women my age feel as "PMZ—Postmenopausal Zest." Mead believed that, after menopause, women could tap into tremendous energy sources to make this period the most exciting one of their lives. She was "high" on middle and old age. And so was I as I sat with my lovely daughter and toasted my "coming of age" (again!) in the dim glow of an elegant restaurant.

But at the same time I was celebrating the end of my child-rearing years, I was aware of the urge to hang on to my children. It was an African border war that consolidated in my mind the need to really let go of my twenty-six-year-old son. On a six-month backpacking trip in Uganda with a friend he was threatened at gunpoint by native soldiers. When a dirty, wrinkled air letter describing the incident arrived weeks later, I was shaken to the core. My firstborn son had experienced a brush with death, and *I hadn't even known about it.* I couldn't have protected him; he was on his own. In the stark realization of that moment I gave up being the protective mother more

Introduction: This Is What Fifty Looks Like!   5

completely than I had done before. My children were adults now. They had no further need for my protection.

Knowing I was no longer needed in that way was a lonely feeling. But there was also a fascination that accompanied the end of my being the family caretaker. With less of my time devoted to doing things for others, more time would be available for me. I could feel the focus shifting; the spotlight was on my life for the first time in more than twenty-five years. And with it came the permission that had never been there before to listen to my own inner voice.

I have spoken with many women who experienced similar moments of realizing that it was time to let their adult children go. As for me, the realization was usually accompanied by a sense of new freedom. And a question: what do I do with it?

When I began listening to the stories of other women, I heard echoes again and again of what had been happening to me. This book was born in those moments of self-discovery as I grew to appreciate how much we can help one another by sharing our experiences, feelings, and fears during this transitional time. In a very real way the stories other women tell serve as guideposts to help lead us through the uncharted territory that lies ahead on the other side of fifty.

❋ ❋

The popular humor about mid-life may help relieve a few of our anxieties about aging, but ultimately this kind of self-ridicule only perpetuates negative stereotypes. While it's true that popular books like Bill Cosby's *Time Flies* are funny, and perhaps not intended to ridicule, they indirectly lend credence to the very myths that need shaking.

How many of us smile agreeably when others blame our moods on the "empty nest syndrome" or "the change"? How many of us allow others to joke about women our age being "all dried up"? And don't most of us accept without question the "fact" that clinical depression is more common among menopausal women than among women of other ages?

For many women, turning fifty has signaled the scariest

transition of their lives, primarily because they have heard so many negatives about it. They have handled the transition in various ways, usually with anxiety or denial. They have laughed, pretending not to be hurt by their portrayal in greeting cards as doddering and senile. The myths, so strong, have beaten many women into submission. Even though these myths so often seem to be out of sync with our deepest experience of life, we are afraid to call them lies.

What are the myths that have turned this age into a time to dread? I find these four to be the most pervasive:

Myth 1: It's Time to Settle Down.

Most people believe that if they have made the right choices their lives at fifty should be winding down into a settled, predictable pattern with few surprises. The women I have interviewed share the opposite feeling. They're *restless*, hungry for new experiences, eager to take chances. Many of them mention having the sensation that there's a "second self" inside, one who has yet to be born and grow. It's another aspect of the "biological clock" that we feel so reborn at this age. I have met a secretary with "a psychic inside" who pursued her interest in astrology only after fifty. Another women returned to school and got her teaching credentials, allowing the "teacher inside" to emerge.

Far from settling down, many women take the bull by the horns and dare to do things they never would have *dreamed* of in their thirties and forties. A softball team I encountered in Amherst, Massachusetts, dubbed the "Hot Flashes," is a feisty gang of menopausal sportswomen who effectively fly balls in the face of myth.

Myth 2: Our Losses Consume Us.

We are apt to fear the empty nest and the possibility of an empty marital bed. We are saddened to see our parents age and know they will not be with us forever. But it is not true that these fears consume or paralyze us. Rather we are so energized by our gains that we refuse to be intimidated by our losses. In his inspiring book *The Road Less Traveled* Dr. Scott Peck notes:

... it is abundantly clear that this lifetime is a series of simultaneous deaths and births. "Throughout the whole of life one must continue to learn to live," said Seneca two millennia ago, "and what will amaze you even more, throughout life one must learn to die." It is also clear that the farther one travels on the journey of life, the more births one will experience, and therefore the more deaths—the more joy and the more pain.

In fact mid-life is not a period that is either particularly perilous *or* particularly serene. It has its own problems and its own rewards—just like every other period in life. And researchers from the University of California, Los Angeles, and Duke University, Durham, North Carolina, have found that the so-called "empty nest syndrome" afflicts fewer people than most people think. According to the researchers, because women are ready for it to happen, we experience our children leaving home as *normal* for this time in our lives.

Myth 3: Life Is One Big Hot Flash.
We have been led to believe that menopause is a time during which every women suffers debilitating and humiliating hot flashes. But recent studies by the University of Utah School of Nursing in Salt Lake City show that less than 10 percent of all women are affected in a dramatic way by hot flashes. The physical symptoms that accompany menopause are real, but the tendency, even among those in the medical profession, to treat this natural life process as a disease (not to mention an embarrassment!) has contributed to the negative way we view one of our most significant life passages.

In the course of interviewing women for this book I encountered many different reactions to the hot flashes and other changes that characterize menopause. Most of the women started with a sense of shame, followed by the fear, if not the downright certainty, that the best years of their sexual lives were behind them. For the most part this is nonsense, but since women tend to keep their menopausal concerns a secret, they often don't have the support that helps them make the transition more easily.

Myth 4: We've Seen It All.

People will say "I may be older, but I'm much wiser," and this is true. But sometimes this wisdom gets glorified and actually encourages stagnation. When you think you've finally got life whipped, you become closed to learning or experiencing new things.

In actuality the women I've interviewed often express surprise that they *don't* know more at fifty. This discovery is mirrored in the thoughtful answer an honors student once gave to the scholarship panel of a prestigious university. The panelists knew that the young woman was from a modest background and that neither of her parents had been educated beyond high school. They asked her to explain how her education had contributed to making her different from her parents. She clinched the scholarship with her answer: "I'm not at all sure I have more answers than my parents do, but I'm positive that I have more questions."

By the time we're fifty we know what we *don't* know. We're wiser to both the dangers and the opportunities. We know that we don't have time for everything and must do the most important things first. But that's different from "having all the answers." The mystery that makes life such an adventure is as great as ever.

I have chosen to delete these myths from my life and pretend that they never existed. They're lies, and when I believe them I feel my progress is halted. What I think you will appreciate most about the opportunity to read about other women our age is the courageous way so many of them have staunchly refused to let the negative myths rule, even when all the evidence seemed to be stacked against them. It is through their eyes that you can begin to look at the world and at your life in a different way. It is difficult to be in the presence of such power and not be deeply influenced by it.

❋ ❋

Alice and Joanne are friends who turned fifty the same year. They had known each other for a long time and had celebrated many birthdays together. As they approached their fiftieth, they often found themselves talking about it. Instead of being embarrassed to be "so old," as one of their daughters put it, they decided to throw a huge party to celebrate their new status. They even talked nine other recently fifty friends into participating in the festivities.

Together the women decided that they would ask their adult children to plan and host the party as a birthday gift. And the children loved the idea. As the plan grew and the preparations took shape, it became an event of far greater magnitude than the two women had ever imagined.

More than 150 people crowded the rented hall on the night of the party. Balloons, streamers, and other festive decorations brightened the room. The centerpiece was a huge cake, adorned with fifty candles. There was dancing, singing, toasting, and gift giving. The evening culminated with the birthday women jointly blowing out the candles on their cake.

Later Alice described in glowing terms her feelings of pride and happiness. "For the first time I really felt *it's great to be fifty*," she said. "I was proud to be standing there in such a prestigious group of women, all of whom had lived for half a century. The combined contribution of that group could never be measured. We certainly had nothing to be ashamed about."

On her fiftieth birthday, Gloria Steinem threw herself a party. When friends complimented her on her youth and energy Steinem laughed. "Take a good look," she said. "This is what fifty looks like!"

When some critics questioned Sally Field's credibility as the mother of a grown daughter in the movie *Steel Magnolias*, the exuberant, youthful Field laughed. "My own children are in their twenties," she said. "This is what mothers of children in their twenties look like."

The concept of rebirth at fifty is no longer such a foreign one in our culture. Some of the most glamorous women of our era have crossed this benchmark—Tina Turner is over fifty. So are Sophia Loren, Shirley MacLaine, and Elizabeth Taylor. Furthermore, there is a growing consensus that true accomplishment becomes possible only as we mature. Margaret Thatcher, perhaps the most powerful woman in the world, is in her sixties. Elizabeth Dole is truly coming into her own as a national figure in her fifties.

It can be uplifting to recognize that beauty, power, and intelligence can be heightened as we age, but most of us struggle to identify with these women. They seem to be so far out of our league. Still, these are the visible models, the women "of a certain age" who today hold high the bright light in a society that still suspects menopausal women of being too dried up to be sexually desirable or too emotionally unstable to have access to the Red Phone.

Little is expected of women at fifty. We are summarily dismissed from any real role, our contribution ended. We inherit the legacy of women from previous generations who viewed this turning point as a period of preparing for the end, not of inventing a new start. There was a practical reason for this. The average life expectancy of a women of my mother's generation, born in 1915, was only 56.8. When my mother reached fifty, she was nearing the end of her expected life span. She felt "old." Today my mother is still alive and healthy at seventy-three. Think of how different the past twenty years might have been for her had she known that she had so many productive years left. Twenty or thirty years is a long time to get ready to die, but many women of her generation did just that.

My mother's life was devoted almost entirely to the role of caretaker. She raised me and my sister, sewed our clothes, cut our hair, presided over our Camp Fire groups, taught Sunday school, cleaned the house, shopped, cooked our meals, redecorated when it was needed. She also took over the role of outdoor gardener and landscaper. I remember her as a very busy woman. But when we left home and my parents moved to a smaller house, her sense of productivity waned for a while until she discovered new gratification through volunteer work.

The women of my mother's generation led productive lives that, more often than not, were not really valued. These were strong, bright, capable women. We all leaned on them and expected them to know how to handle every crisis. But their strength, while taken for granted, was never fully appreciated. And as they aged, even their limited value depreciated.

In *Passages*, her famous book on life changes, written in 1976, Gail Sheehy describes the period of fifty and over as "... old age, a time set aside primarily to accept one's mortality."

How odd that seems to us now, a scant fourteen years later. Sentiments like these leave us with the strong sensation of not "feeling fifty." We can no longer identify with the way our mothers, their friends, and society defined (and continue to define) this age. Using their criteria, I would say I feel thirty. Many of my contemporaries agree.

And yet we're not thirty. We *are* fifty. The facts can't be altered. What we *can* do is rewrite the script for what being fifty means. We can lift the weight of depression from aging and adopt a new paradigm for the change of life. We can celebrate the fact that we are in the midst of a longevity revolution; demographers predict that by the middle of the next century people could very well live to be 130. I predict that when I reach eighty I will feel the way my mother felt at fifty.

Rather than marking the end of life, fifty actually marks the midpoint of adult life, with many years of healthy, productive time stretched before us. Joanne Stevenson, an Ohio State University professor who studied middle-aged and elderly populations, described it well when she called the period between the ages of fifty and seventy "middlescence." Stevenson pointed out that most people continue to grow emotionally and intellectually well into their seventies. "Middle-agers shouldn't be considered elderly until this time," said Stevenson. "From my observations there is a transition and some kind of deterioration between seventy and eighty, but rarely before that. What makes a vital person retire at sixty-two or sixty-five?"

Although many psychologists and sociologists are of the opinion that age fifty is the beginning of a time of "disengagement" (the natural preparation for old age and death), my conversations with women show that they are more *engaged* than ever. Rather than pulling away from friends and friendship, they are embracing them with a new vigor that increased free time now makes possible. In her book *Among Friends*, Letty Cottin Pogrebin describes the period between ages forty and sixty-five as a time when people are "downshifting from career overdrive and making time for friends."

If anything is different about our intimacies, it is that we are more selective. We no longer hold on to people just because they like us; we want to be with people *we* like. This refocusing is probably due to the important lessons we've learned about love, as well as to the realization that there is no time to waste. On the home stretch every moment counts.

But making every moment count is not the same as being in what I call "the last-chance corral." Since society has favored the view that nothing much is achieved after fifty, there tends to be a desperate plunge (or "mid-life crisis") in the years leading up to fifty.

A professional women in her late forties related a sense of desperation when she told me this story: "The last time I attended a bar association meeting an old friend approached me, an incredibly handsome man whom I have been attracted to for years. He asked me out for a drink, and one thing led to another. On the dance floor of a club where we finally ended up at two in the morning, he asked me to go back to his hotel room. I said no, but I'll tell you, as I get closer to fifty, I feel more and more that I should take advantage of offers like that. After all, once I turn fifty I won't have the chance anymore."

She may be wrong! It has been said that growing old is a process we really begin at birth. We do not wake up on our fiftieth birthday to find that we have aged. The date does not mark the end of our desirability or our capability. There's only one "last chance"—it is the moment we take our final breath. The time before that is called *living*.

※ ※

The idea for this book was inspired by the growing awareness that we fifty-year-old women are at a pivotal point in life's journey. And yet the positive aspects of turning fifty (and the reasons to celebrate this important milestone) are seldom articulated. As I began to interview women about their experiences, I found that many seemed shy about relating any hint of exhilaration, as though others would consider it phony. One woman spoke for many when she observed, "It's so easy to get carried along by the negative sentiments. People expect you to feel bad about turning fifty, so you accommodate them. And if you do try to express any happiness with being your age, people look at you with pity, thinking you're only trying to be brave in the face of a miserable situation." This woman's remark spoke to the need for a new way of telling the turning-fifty story, and that is what I set out to do with this book.

To gather material I interviewed at least two hundred women between the ages of forty-seven and fifty-four. The basis for our conversations was the set of questions I developed on the subject (see Appendix B). Topics ranged from their experience of sexuality at mid-life to the new choices they were pursuing in their careers.

In addition I held several group sessions in different cities, wanting to see if women across the nation shared similar experiences. These gatherings, which took place in Minneapolis, New Orleans, Los Angeles, Hartford, and Westchester, New York, were powerful, affirmative events. I had already concluded that women of our age did not talk much to one another about their true experiences, fears, and hopes. I viewed the group process as a magic box that would be opened to reveal all manner of intriguing and inspiring details. And, indeed, this turned out to be true, as you will find when you read the accounts of these conversations.

In writing this book I am allowing the women of my generation to have their turn. Their stories, ideas, and reflections, spoken with rare honesty and insight, can serve as guideposts for other women. For although each woman's experience is in many ways unique, collectively they impart wisdom about what I have come to regard as universal concerns of women our age. Indeed it is heartening to find that there are creative ways of dealing with the issues we face.

Nearly every women I spoke with mentioned how good it felt to learn that she was not alone, that her feelings and experiences were shared by others. It is my hope that, reading this book, you will begin to see yourself too as part of this wonderful, vibrant community of women, who have many years of important contributions to make and happy times to share.

1
A New Way to Act Our Age

"I've been thinking about birthdays lately—specifically, the way women celebrate turning fifty," I said to the small group of women sitting around me in a circle. At my urging my friend Martha had arranged this gathering of women she knew, in Hartford, Connecticut, who had turned fifty during the past two years. There was an upbeat, almost giddy feeling in the air, an immediate sense of intimacy. "This is fun," said Martha, who in casual jeans and a sweater looked slim and attractive. "It reminds me of the consciousness-raising sessions I used to go to fifteen years ago. Remember those?"

"Oh, yes," I smiled. "We outgrew them, but nothing ever took their place. Do you realize how unusual it is for a group of women to meet and talk about things like this?"

"Sometimes I'll get together for dinner or drinks with one or two girlfriends," said Linda, a fifty-year-old lawyer who had been divorced two years earlier. "We always have a good time, but some subjects are off-limits, and age is one of them. I was quite surprised when Martha invited me to come tonight."

"I'm sure we're all familiar with the stereotype of the woman who stops having birthdays at the age of thirty-nine," I said. "Even many women who admit to being fifty would find the idea of *celebrating* it outrageous. A lot of them would rather not think about it at all."

"It wouldn't be such an outrageous idea if we didn't idolize youth so much in our society," said Martha. "People act like you should be embarrassed about growing older. So we end up being ashamed to admit we're turning fifty."

"Or we joke about it," I added. "Lately I've been looking at birthday cards, and it's very hard to find cards for fifty-year-old women that aren't disparaging in some way." I held up a sample. "Here's one that shows an old dowager-type lady on the front who looks like she's about eighty. She's saying 'There's something to be said about turning fifty.' Then you open it up and get the punch line: 'It sucks.'" Everyone groaned. I held up a second card. "Here's one that says 'Don't worry about this birthday . . . fifty isn't old . . .' And inside it says, 'If you're a tree.'"

Corinne, an attractive fifty-one-year-old in a powder-blue warm-up suit, threw up her hands, exasperated. "Who are they designing those cards for? They make me angry."

"Here's the worst one," I continued, pulling out a third card. "It says 'Some birthday riddles for your fiftieth birthday . . . How many fifty-year-olds does it take to change a light bulb?' The answer? 'None. They prefer it dark. Better for napping.'"

The four women grimaced.

I shrugged. "But who's surprised? I'll bet you all got at least a couple of cards like that when you turned fifty."

Linda laughed. "I've been getting cards like that since I turned thirty! The greeting card sections are full of them. I think the only age it's okay for a woman to be is sixteen . . . or maybe twenty-one."

"So," I continued, "having said all that, you know I'm very curious about how you celebrated your fiftieth birthdays. Celebrating fifty, as I said before, is a very difficult idea for some people to grasp. When I first began talking to publishers about this book, many of them just shook their heads in complete lack of comprehension. One marketing executive—a man, I might add—said, 'I don't see women buying this book and carrying it around in public. They wouldn't want people to know they were fifty.' But meanwhile I was hearing an entirely different story from the women themselves. I'm not suggesting that there's something magic that happens at fifty. But those people who think it's a great trauma might be surprised to hear about all the positive aspects of this age. Quite a few women have told me about feeling wonderful—about wanting to celebrate. Even those who feel ambivalent are often aware that there's something very significant about this milestone."

"I was thinking about not celebrating it—just kind of letting it slide past," admitted Linda. "It's funny how something as seemingly insignificant as turning a year older can work such a trip on your head, but I was really dreading it more and more as the big day got closer. I kept thinking, 'This is it, I'm old now.' I was surprised about how much I thought about my mortality, probably because my mother was so much older at fifty than I—I never thought I would be that old. I was also feeling a little sorry for myself because I'm divorced and I had always taken it for granted that by the time I hit fifty I would be settled down. Fortunately I had a couple of very dear friends who had both turned fifty several years before me, and they said, 'We'll help you through.' One came from out of state to visit me. She was determined that I wouldn't celebrate alone, because she knew how hard it could be to get through it. I'm sure this support was part of the reason my mental attitude turned completely around. When I woke up on my birthday, I felt like I was reborn. I had this wonderful feeling, like 'This is the second half of my life—it starts today.' It turned out to be a very upbeat, celebratory day. The people at work gave me a surprise party and took me out to lunch. There were funny gifts and champagne and craziness all day long. And the man I've been seeing took me out for a beautiful dinner.

"But the best part was the day after my birthday. My daughter asked me to stop by her apartment on my way home from work. We planned to share a pizza and just talk. I walked in, and it was a surprise party. The apartment was decorated with banners and fifty balloons that covered her living room ceiling. My three children and my friends were all there, and everyone was wearing birthday hats that said 'It's Nifty to Be Fifty.' And get this. When my daughter brought out the cake, everyone took out tiny harmonicas and played 'Happy Birthday' on them." She flushed, remembering her pleasure. "It was a great outpouring of love."

Martha said, "That sounds perfect. I'm convinced that it's much better to celebrate than to keep it inside. If you don't share it, you'll just turn your feelings inward and become negative. A few weeks before my birthday I started to get hot flashes during the day. It was so embarrassing, and the timing was lousy—it just reinforced the feeling I was getting old. But my son showed up a couple of days before my birthday with two crates of wine, one red and one white, and clearly his message was 'Good for you—let's celebrate.' And my husband, who is fifty-seven, thinks I look great, so that perked me up, too."

I nodded. "It's almost as though turning fifty happens in stages. First comes the dread that you both described, then almost an exhilaration."

"My birthday was fun," recalled Corinne. "I planned to have my four children over in the evening for a quiet celebration. But they arrived with decorations, refreshments, and a cake, and made me sit down and relax while they set things up. Suddenly, people started walking in the door, and I realized that my husband and children had arranged a surprise party. I felt very proud and special."

"What about you, Sylvia?" I asked.

I had known Sylvia, a fifty-two-year-old interior decorator with a son away at college and a teenage daughter, almost as long as I had known Martha. She has always been one of those energetic, organized women who seem to effortlessly keep several plates spinning in the air at once. "My party was great too, because I threw it for myself," she said.

"Two years ago my whole family forgot my birthday," she

explained, "and I was certainly not going to let that happen again, especially for such an important year. Besides, this way I was able to have everything exactly the way I wanted. I invited only people I liked—no business associates or those people you always invite to parties because they invite you to their parties but who are not really friends. I hired a caterer and someone to clean my house, and then I sat back and waited for people to come and bring me presents." She leaned back against the pillows and smiled with satisfaction.

"There was a great mix of people there," said Sylvia. "Everyone made a real effort to come. They seemed to appreciate the importance of the event. Before dessert I served champagne, and I toasted them, my friends. It felt very significant, a real milestone. I was half a century old!"

Corinne grimaced. "Half a century. I can't get over it."

"One of the reasons we find it hard to believe we're fifty is that we feel and act much younger than our mothers did at this age," I said. "And fifty doesn't mean being old anymore. Women's life expectancy has increased dramatically. Most of us have twenty, thirty, or even more years of active life to look forward to. It's definitely a transition into a new period, not a decline. I've been asking women—and why don't we try this?—how old they actually feel. Your biological ages are over fifty, but what is your psychological age?"

"About thirty-five," Martha said immediately.

"I feel my age—fifty-two." Sylvia shrugged. "Whatever that feels like." We laughed.

Corinne considered the question. "I guess I feel about forty-four."

"It depends," said Linda. "Some days I feel about fifty-five. On my good days I feel forty."

"Now think about this. If you were going to draw a life line with the starting point being birth and the ending point being death, where would you put yourself on the line? In other words, do you feel as though you have lived half your life, more than half, or less than half?"

"Less than half," said Martha bravely. "I had two great-aunts who lived into their nineties. I'm definitely planning to top one hundred."

"I agree with Martha," said Corinne. "I don't feel like I've reached the halfway mark yet."

"Oh, goodness, I have." Sylvia's face registered shock at the idea of living for another fifty years. "I would put myself at about the two-thirds mark. That gives me another twenty-five years, which seems like a lot of time to me."

"Maybe a little more than half," said Linda. "I could see living until I'm in my eighties or nineties."

"In fact fifty is literally a halfway point," I said. "If you divide your adult life into two parts, you'll see that. The first half is between twenty and fifty, and the second half is between fifty and eighty. I think looking at the timeline adds some perspective to what being fifty means."

"It's thrilling in a way," said Linda. "When you consider that most of us grew up with the idea that we would be old by the time we reached fifty, it's like having life given back to us."

"Well," I said, "now that you have all decided that you're going to live so long, let's talk about what you're going to do with all this time."

"For me thinking about the future is really opening up a can of worms," admitted Martha seriously.

"How so?"

"My husband and I seem to have different agendas for the coming years. We've been married since we were eighteen, and this has never happened before. I'm not sure what to do about it. I want to keep doing what I'm doing, but my husband is getting ready to retire in three years." She sighed. "I spent most of my adult life raising five kids and being a perfect wife and mother. Ed always promised me that when our youngest graduated from high school he would support me in finishing my education and pursuing whatever career I wanted. He's been great about it. I went back and got my degree, and now I've been a practicing psychotherapist for four years, and I just love it. Anyway, now that I've shifted gears and started to develop myself professionally, he's suddenly got to retire in three years."

"So, let him retire," said Linda. "That doesn't mean you can't keep practicing."

"That's the problem. He wants to travel. He just bought a boat, and he has this idea that he wants to sail it down to Florida and live on it part of the time. It's not exactly the kind of setting where I could do clinical work." She waved a hand in a gesture of defeat. "So, that's that. I guess I can imagine being happy doing it—I've always been happy doing whatever he wanted. It just wasn't what I had planned."

"I feel for you, Martha," I said. "It's traumatic when people like you and Ed, who have been so close for more than thirty years, suddenly discover that you're on different tracks. After a time the closeness gets taken for granted. You begin to assume things about one another, and it can be a real jolt to suddenly find that you want different things. Have you thought about what you're going to do?"

She shook her head. "I try not to think about it too much. I'll probably do it, though. For all these years Ed has done such a good job of working hard and taking care of the family. I think he deserves this, and it wouldn't be fair for me to stand in the way. I've always told him, 'Wherever you go, I will go.' You know, all these years when he's had to get up and go to a job every day, I've had lots of flexibility. I could go to the beach with the kids or take naps in the afternoon or just curl up and read a book if I wanted to. He's never had a chance to do that."

"You've never had a chance to pursue your career until now."

"Yes, that's true. Look—I have three more years. Maybe I'll be tired of this in three years. It's hard work, and the hours are long. Right now I'm trying to live pretty much for the moment. It's silly to waste time thinking about how unhappy I might be in a few years."

"But," argued Corinne, "if you don't think about it, you might end up being shocked when it's time to go. If it were me, I think I'd feel bitter."

Sylvia laughed suddenly. "I'll tell you what, Martha. One of my dreams is to travel. Why don't I go with Ed? You can stay here with my husband." Everyone roared with laughter, and the tension in the room was broken.

Martha laughed too, but then she grew serious. "Actually that's part of the problem. There are so many women who *would* go with him, without a second thought. If I take a stand, I might be putting my marriage at risk."

"Maybe there are options you haven't considered," Linda suggested. "My husband and I faced the same problem three years ago. For a while I thought we'd end up in a divorce because I refused to think about retirement and giving up my career just because *he* was ready to retire. We talked about our different needs a lot, and we were both scared to death that we wouldn't be able to find a compromise. But as time passed, we both began to see ways we could get our needs met."

"How did you do it?" asked Martha. "Sometimes it seems so impossible to think that we could reach a meeting of the minds about this."

Linda nodded. "I know what you mean. I felt that way, too, for a long time. It took a while. One thing that happened was my husband realized he didn't really want to retire yet—he just wanted a change. He took on a new business and put off retirement for a year or two. During that time, I found that I was changing too. I started doing things that weren't directly related to my career—like developing my interests in gardening and flower arranging. Now we're talking about moving. We don't think of it as retiring exactly, but rather as a chance to do something together in a new place. We've been taking our vacations in various cities to find the one we like best, and I think we've settled on Santa Fe, New Mexico. I guess the point is that we each wanted so much to stay together and make it work that we both made compromises. And we gave it time, so neither of us would feel that we were making a big sacrifice."

"It's not always perfectly clear what choice one should make," I said. "You want to be true to yourself, but sometimes you're not sure who that self is."

"How do you find out?" Linda wondered.

"Asking yourself how you would be living if you had only

one year left is a good way to check out how true you're being to yourself," I suggested.

"I did that," said Sylvia. "I said, 'I'd wear more rhinestones.' So now I've started wearing more rhinestones."

Everyone laughed. "That's our Sylvia," joked Linda. "She cuts straight to the bone."

"For me," said Martha, "I think there are a lot of wonderful possibilities. There's probably at least one more career in me. Sometimes I imagine myself in living arrangements with other women—kind of a 'Golden Girls' type of existence."

"I agree," said Sylvia. "I love the idea of living with friends—of sisterhood. It's comforting to think about. I certainly don't want my children to have to take care of me—physically or financially."

We talked some more about the future, and I could see that all the women in the room had given a lot of thought to the years ahead, building secret plans for the time when they would no longer be caretakers of children and parents.

"I have been meeting with a group of women on a regular basis for about two years," added Corinne. "The group started because we were all interested in learning how to invest in stocks. We made quite a bit of money in the market, and now we're talking about buying a large piece of land and building our own town-house community, which, for now, we'll share with our husbands. But it has occurred to us that some of our husbands may die before us, and it might eventually become a community of women."

"How does this plan change the way you view the future?" I asked.

"Well, there's less anxiety," Corinne said. "I've never been able to picture the future before, and it has bothered me. Now, there's something to look forward to, and I'm actually excited about it. Mostly, I no longer have the fear that I'll end up with my children having to take care of me, or worse, in a nursing home."

"It's funny," mused Sylvia. "When I was a young girl, I used to daydream about being married, having children—how wonderful it would be to take care of a family. And it has been wonderful. But now my daydreams are about myself and all the interesting adventures I'm going to have."

"We can be trapped by the notion that we have only one chance in life," I told them. "That the road not taken is the road lost forever. In our society we are not accustomed to thinking of life as a series of stages, each one bringing a new direction and a different kind of fulfillment. If you really examine your thoughts, you might find that you are embarrassed to admit your most precious dreams—as though it's wrong somehow for women our age to have dreams."

I suspected that Martha's dilemma was not uncommon. We assume that we will progress through the life stages hand in hand with our husbands, and many women are unprepared for the conflicting goals that emerge during this period. When I began to ask women about the subject of their husbands' retirement, I found that they often faced unexpected conflicts. Jody, a writer in her late forties married to a man fourteen years her senior, expressed how frustrating it had been for her since her husband had retired. "During the week my home is my office," she told me. "I have work to do. But Ed doesn't get that. He'll come in while I'm writing and say 'Let's go play tennis' or 'Let's go out to lunch.' When I tell him I can't because I'm working, he can't understand. He feels rejected. It's so ironic—and maddening! I feel as though I'm really at my prime, workwise. I want to immerse myself in my writing. And Ed is winding down."

Helen Bennett, a Connecticut writer, expressed similar frustrations in an article for the *New York Times Magazine* entitled, "Two of Us Is One Too Many." She wrote, "He was a prowler on my turf and I hated it. When my husband took early retirement, I came down with a late, hard case of culture shock. It made me crazy. Surely, it would have made him crazy if I had hung around his office all day asking, 'Is it late to eat lunch?' 'Are you ready for the meeting tomorrow?'" Bennett's husband eventually got tired of the leisure and found a new job that he enjoyed, thus solving the problem. But Bennett admitted to having mixed feelings about the entire matter. She remembered a time, and it did not seem that long ago, when her husband had been so involved in his work that she felt abandoned. Now she felt ridiculous for complaining that he was present too much. The experience taught her a lot about what she really wanted.

The men in our lives have their own set of struggles at this stage of life. Unfortunately couples aren't always in sync, either sexually or in other arenas. I've spoken with many women who feel that they are just starting to come into their own in their careers—or who are returning to work now that their children are grown. But their husbands are starting to wind down. They've had their careers, and now they want something different. The myth is that when you love someone you're always going to be at the same place, but it *is* a myth. And men in their fifties can be easily threatened. The younger men are coming up at work and pushing them aside. They may not feel as sexually confident as they once did. Sometimes they respond to their insecurity by exerting tighter control over their families or by becoming too needy.

I am reminded of an older friend whose doctor prescribed estrogen therapy, and she came flying home to her husband, full of excitement. She told him about the estrogen. "My doctor says I'll feel a lot less tired," she said. "He says it'll be like I'm so much younger." Her husband looked at her in horror and replied, "How much younger are you going to be?"

I do not mean to suggest that men and women our age are always out of sync or that the subject of retirement is always a battleground. I met other women who went through this phase without trauma, whose desires *were* in sync with those of their husbands. But overall I found that today's fifty-year-old woman is not winding down—far from it. Most of the women I spoke with told me of feeling new freedom, of discovering long-buried talents, of finally having a chance to pursue careers and take new risks. Whereas their more traditional husbands were slowing down to take advantage of a leisure they felt that long years of work had entitled them to, the wives were running full steam ahead.

Often the men were bewildered by this new energy. "This is the time when we should be slowing down," they said. Or "Act your age—you're a grandmother now." For them the word *retirement* inspired visions of freedom, but for many women it seemed to mean just the opposite, a suffocating, deadening decline into old age.

Many women expressed to me their concerns about structured retirement communities as a possibility for later in their lives. The most common concern was that living in a structured community of older people might isolate them from the mainstream. As one woman noted, "I can see the advantages, in that they can prevent people from being totally alone in their later years. But I wonder if I might feel isolated just the same. All the positive images I have created for myself about growing older have placed me in the center of a full community, where I interact daily with men, women, and children of all ages."

While I did speak with women who were looking forward to retirement and the freedom it implied, most of them viewed it as an opportunity for a level of creativity and activism for which they had not previously had time. Their feelings about retirement communities ranged from lukewarm to outright distaste. "I like the idea of being part of a larger group," said one woman. "But I picture an environment more like the Israeli kibbutz, where people of all ages live and work together. I don't want to live in a community where there are no children." Another woman, echoing this sentiment, raised the question "What kind of children will we raise if they are cut off from the older generation?"

Finally, the real questions are: What kind of people will we be in our later years? What will our lifestyles look like? What will it mean to act our age?

※ ※

Most of us grow up believing the maturity myth. One idea emanating from this myth is that if you make the right choices as a young adult you will be home safe by your forties—that choosing the correct path when you are in your twenties will guarantee your fulfillment for the rest of your life.

In this antiquated conception of life stages adulthood is the dormant period that lies beneath the growth stage of youth and the winding-down stage of our senior years. It is the time when the least amount of upheaval is believed to occur.

Not only are we told that we will be home free if we settle down and organize our lives around an approved set of external goals; we are also promised that once we settle down we will become less restless and more stable. In our rush to become what we are led to believe is "mature," we often make decisions before we have much knowledge of ourselves or insight into the realities of the future. A student who has not chosen a career by the third year of college is considered a failure, yet one who has set his or her sights firmly in one direction has inadequate experience to make a decision that is supposed to guarantee a lifetime of success and personal fulfillment.

We are promised that by settling into a marriage we will attain emotional security. However, the reality of the divorce rate seems to indicate that the mate we choose at twenty might not be around to provide us emotional security at thirty. We never stop changing, and we sometimes outgrow the choices we made for ourselves when we were younger.

Another aspect of the maturity myth is that once we have grown up and settled down, our sex life will be safe. We won't have to worry about it anymore. However, again reality seems to refute this assumption. The vast popularity of sex manuals, the estimates indicating that at least one partner suffers from sexual dysfunction in nearly 50 percent of American marriages, and the prevalence of such phenomena as exchanging partners, group sex, and pornographic movies seem to indicate that a great number of people have failed to find the sexual safety or satisfaction they thought marriage would bring them.

And finally, the maturity myth leads us to believe that, if we settle down, the future will become manageable. However, in reality, it is clear that we can't be certain about that either. The future remains a highly unpredictable quantity—no matter what we do.

When we view "settling down" as the major goal of adulthood, we assume that we will continue to be satisfied with the same goals and values for the next fifty years that we established in our twenties. But what if we don't, in fact, want the same things even ten or twenty years later?

Any major change in adulthood is viewed with suspicion. And yet the very act of living forces a constant change. If we are to maintain our self-esteem, not to mention our sanity, we must invent a new way of defining maturity.

The only thing that is predictable about adulthood is that it is unpredictable. The excitement of adulthood comes from our willingness to take risks, not just use all of our energy trying to avoid crises.

Ironically, many women have reported to me that they feel ashamed of their fantasies about the future. As one woman told me, "I like it that my children are grown and no longer live at home, but I feel guilty about liking it. Aren't mothers supposed to hate it when their children leave?" Another woman, divorced in her early fifties, admitted that she looked forward to going out again and having an active social life. "But I don't ever say this to my children. I have a feeling they would think it inappropriate. I can hear their voices in my head, chiding 'Act your age, Mother.'"

But what does it mean to act our age—this age? We're familiar with the stereotypes: start slowing down, dress conservatively, cut your hair short, stay home and wait for the grandchildren to visit, and, most important of all, hide any indication that you are still interested in sex. We are also familiar with the reverse stereotype—what I call the "Golden Girls" syndrome: Go out and kick up your heels, have lots of sexual adventures, behave in a silly, outrageous, slightly batty manner, and prove to the world that you're still "young at heart."

Neither of these stereotypes rings true for the vast majority of women. Elizabeth Taylor might have appeared to be an endearing symbol of youth as she rode on the back of Malcolm

Forbes's motorcycle, but I'm not about to start "kicking up my heels" all of a sudden. And how many of us have long hours to spend baking cookies for the grandchildren? We are, by and large, busy, involved women. Many of us are just hitting our stride professionally, or starting new careers, or going back to school. We don't worry endlessly about how to act, as though the change of life required a change of personality as well. We do worry about how we look, but we're not as consumed with looking young, necessarily, as we are with looking good.

"I get angry about the way women our age are portrayed on television," Shirley, a fifty-two-year-old marketing executive told me. "There are some pretty good examples of women at forty—it's okay to be forty now. But when you get to fifty, forget it. What do we have? An eccentric woman detective and a group of giddy women who behave like adolescents. And I won't even mention how the soap operas denigrate older women. I don't feel much different from the way I felt ten years ago, and I don't really look much different, either. If anything, I'm more experienced and capable now. I feel better about myself than I did when I was younger."

In *Age Wave—The Challenges and Opportunities of an Aging America*, Ken Dychtwald, Ph.D., says that the way we respond to aging depends to a great extent on the way we think about aging. And, Dychtwald suggests, this has a lot to do with our cultural environment. "When asked, 'How old are you?' a 55-year-old in China might cheat a bit and claim to be 59," writes Dychtwald. "But an American asked the same question would be more likely to respond with 'I never tell my age' or to cheat a bit and answer, 'I'm 49.'"

Dychtwald, who is one of the nation's leading activists against ageism, points out that we do not have to feel doomed to parrot culturally inspired ideas that are no longer relevant, and herein lies the key to our futures. Cultural stereotypes are changed when people invent new paradigms, and this is a process in which each of us plays a role. We can begin, I believe, by refusing to become caricatures, either of the grandmother-fifty or of the swinging-fifty. What it means to look and act our age probably is little different from when we were in our forties.

Women will also be responsible for redefining the concept of retirement, for we refuse to be put out to pasture. We will find a new word for those later years that communicates our full involvement in the world and our intention to be at the center of things, in one way or another, until we die.

WHAT DOES FIFTY MEAN TO YOU?

One of the ways to feel empowered as you reach your fiftieth year is to examine what this age means to you. Most of us have little to guide us but other people's impressions of what this age means. You may feel that these impressions have little to do with the way you really look and feel, but you have trouble expressing the identifying factors that make this age special for you.

I have found that the exercise I used with the group earlier in this chapter has been successful in helping women find what I call their psychological age. And it is your psychological age—that point in your life you believe you've reached—that counts the most. It is far more meaningful to what you ultimately decide to do with your life than is your chronological age.

You can do this exercise yourself by drawing a "life line" on a piece of paper, the beginning of the line representing your birth and the end of the line your death.

Life Line

X————————————————————————X
birth   death

Mark an X on the point of your life line where you would place yourself today. Do you believe that you have lived half your life? Less than half? More than half?

Now draw a second line to represent your adult life, the beginning of the line representing the beginning of your adulthood at age twenty. Mark an X on the point at which you believe yourself to be in your adult life. Have you lived half your adult years? Less than half? More than half? Do you see yourself as being near the end of adulthood?

Adult Life

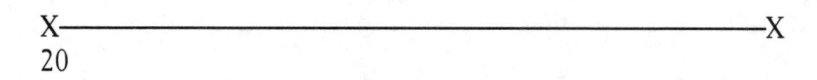

X———————————————————————X
20

What does your response to this exercise tell you? I've conducted it with many women, and the most common reaction is surprise that they find so much possibility remaining in their lives. Performing this exercise is a graphic way to remind yourself that, at fifty, you need not feel that you are in your waning years. It is also the first step toward thinking about what kind of mark you want to make in the twenty, thirty, or even forty years that lie ahead of you. When you place yourself on the life line, you are making a decision that your life is equally valid at every phase. Your vitality is not diminished by your age.

If you like, you can take this exercise one step further and give a name to the phase of life you are now entering. For example, you may call the coming years a time of exploration, if it is your plan to travel; community might be another focus, if you're planning to make a special effort to be connected to others by becoming more involved in your community; or maybe your focus will be an artistic expression or religious renewal.

Recently I helped one of my patients identify herself on a lifeline. This woman, who was in her early fifties, identified the first phase of her adulthood as "mothering." With her children now grown, she needed to find a new way to identify who she was, and she chose to name this period in her life that of "activist," because she planned to get involved in community organizations that she had previously not had time for. The process of creating an overriding theme for her middle years was a breakthrough experience. As she put it, "It gave me a way of understanding this time in my life as a point of beginning rather than a time of ending."

The well-worn adage that "today is the first day of the rest of your life" takes on special meaning when you stand up and take account of yourself, when you shake off the crusty old images that imply your best years are past. Living fully as a woman of fifty means inventing for yourself a way to be and placing your own signature on the years ahead.

❋ 2 ❋
Affirming the Change of Life

It was twilight in Minneapolis, and I sat with a group of five women in a restaurant overlooking the city, watching the lights slowly flicker on below. We had just ordered dinner and now were talking about aging and the experience of menopause. All agreed that they felt younger than their years, that the fifty landmark had sneaked up on them and caught them off guard. I told them that their observations echoed those I had been hearing from women all over the country.

"We don't really have many role models for what it looks and feels like to be fifty," I said. "We think we know what it's supposed to be like, but our own experiences don't fit the images we have. They certainly don't fit the concept that, at this time in our lives, we should be winding down. And when we look in the mirror, we don't see old women. Most women I've spoken with feel that they look younger than what they think fifty should look like. Because we lack the role models, the concept of being this age and of going through menopause can be very confusing and scary."

Carol, a tall, slim woman of forty-nine who was letting her short brown hair go gray, nodded in agreement. "My mother was a very unhappy person at mid-life. She had so much energy, but she had nothing to do with it, because she had never considered herself as having a role apart from raising her kids. I made up my mind a long time ago, watching her, that it wasn't going to be that way for me. But even though my life is very different, I find that being this age is harder and more confusing than I had expected. I wish I had someone who could tell me how I'm supposed to feel and what the experience of menopause is supposed to be like."

Marilyn, a petite, pretty blond woman of fifty, who had been divorced four years earlier, nodded vigorously in agreement. "I never wanted to be like my mother, either. She was this nice, loving lady, but she just wasn't interested in what was going on around her. She was too limited in her scope—she was only a mother, and that defined her totally. I always knew that I would grow older in a different way than she did."

"We are not like our mothers," said June, a youthful blond fifty-year-old. "My mother's life was so sheltered. She was trapped in this situation with my father. Her role was to serve him, and it was clear that would always be her role. She wasn't free. She had nothing of her own. She was relentlessly married, relentlessly suburban, relentlessly Christian, relentlessly a cook." She laughed. "I guess you could say she was relentlessly a negative role model."

Rarely did the women I interviewed name their own mothers as positive role models for this period in their lives, evidence, no doubt, that a tremendous generational change had occurred during the past twenty to thirty years. We were being called on to serve as the pioneers of a new definition of the mature woman. The thought never failed to fill the women I met with excitement—but it was scary too.

"How about you, Naomi?" I turned to the woman on my right, who had not yet spoken. Naomi was a jewelry designer of fifty-two whose long, silver-streaked black hair was tied in a braid behind her head.

"I guess I have to say that I'm one of the rare ones whose mother has been a good role model. She's eighty-four years old, and she's still going strong. In fact, it has only been in the last year that she has started to slow down a little. When she was fifty, she still seemed young to me, although there were fewer opportunities available to her then than there are for me now."

"What do you think makes your mother different from so many other women of her age?" I asked.

Naomi shrugged. "Maybe it's that she never believed that growing older meant being elderly. It's an attitude that she has—there's always something interesting out there. The learning never stops."

"Isn't that kind of attitude something people either have or don't?" wondered Carol. "I know people who are thirty years old, and they think they've already seen all there is to see of life. On the other hand my father's mother was a lot like Naomi's mother. She started working in the 1920s, and when she got divorced she supported her family. She was ahead of her time in that respect. I idolized her. She was funny and interesting, and she had a boyfriend. When I was a child, they would take me for rides in his motorcar. I remember my grandmother always looked so beautiful sitting next to him in the car. She wore great hats and nice suits and lots of makeup."

"I think my mother wanted things to be different," said June. "She had internalized values that were good, but she didn't have any permission to take on a new role. Her whole message to me was 'Don't let anyone know you exist.' And my whole thing has always been 'Here I am.' We're very different."

"Even when our own mothers did not serve as role models, many women can point to another adult woman or women in our lives—teachers, a neighbor, another relative—who served that role," I observed. "Can you think of any women who did this for you?"

"The nuns who ran my college were pretty radical for their time," said Carol. "I admired them so much because they were the first women I had ever met who seemed to be doing exactly what they wanted to do. Even though their lives were structured, they seemed far more independent than my mother."

"I had someone too," said Marilyn, smiling. "My aunt—my father's sister—was single, which everyone thought was shocking at that time. She lived in Washington, D.C., and she used to visit us once a year. She was so stylish and interesting. She finally did marry—when she was sixty-two! Now that I think about it, it was her being single that impressed me so much. I viewed my own mother as stuck, and Aunt Ruth wasn't stuck at all."

"It's important for us to be aware of the ways our mothers dealt with their menopausal years, because it explains a lot of our mixed feelings about being this age," I said. "When our mothers were fifty, we thought of them as old and they thought of themselves as old. Their focus was shifting down, and they believed the best years of their lives were over. It's very different for us. For one thing, menopause signals the end of our childbearing years, but as women we are no longer defined solely by our role as mothers. We are more likely to see our lives as a series of transitions from one stage to another.

"This change of life is not just happening physically," I continued. "It touches all arenas of our lives. And yet the physical signs, because they are the most tangible, are the ones that we give the greatest attention. Unfortunately the idea of menopause is loaded with negative connotations. It is the secret scourge of women, something we rarely even talk about among ourselves. We don't know what to expect. It scares us and makes us vulnerable to the suggestion that we're not in the right state of mind to make decisions during this period. We don't know what's normal."

Joyce, a well-tailored woman of fifty-two with beautiful smooth skin, nodded vigorously in agreement. "Menopause is the most embarrassing time of life," she said. "I don't think I've ever heard anything good about it. People—especially men—think you're drying up. Who wants to talk about it? My attitude is to *just get through it*."

"Let's talk about it now," I suggested, and the women shifted uncomfortably around the table. There was a long silence before Joyce broke the ice by joking, "See what I mean?

Nobody wants to talk about it. It's worse than going to the dentist."

"Why do you suppose we're so embarrassed about a natural change of life?" I wondered aloud.

"It makes sense," said Carol. "For me there was the same sense of secrecy when I first got my period. My mother never told me in advance what to expect. She was embarrassed by it, so it made me feel embarrassed too. When she got older, she never mentioned menopause. I worried about hot flashes, and I started reading nutritional books because I heard somewhere that if you had the right nutritional program you wouldn't need estrogen. But I did this on my own. I didn't talk to anyone about it. When I started missing my periods and experiencing other symptoms, I didn't even tell my husband. I guess I didn't want him to think of me as being that old."

"When I told a friend that I took my daughter out to dinner to celebrate the beginning of my menopause," I said, "she was horrified. Even people who profess to have a so-called 'modern' view don't want to hear the details. As a result, women our age often feel stranded. There's an important change happening, but they can't discuss it with anyone."

"I'm going to say something embarrassing," Joyce said, looking down at the table. "I mean, it's embarrassing to me. I don't know why, but I've always been embarrassed about menstruation. I *blush* if the subject comes up. For thirty years, I hid my tampons from my husband. I never mentioned my period. There were a few days during the month when sex was off-limits, as far as I was concerned, but I never said 'I'm having my period.' What was I thinking—that maybe he wouldn't guess I menstruated? I hate the fact that I've done that, but when you said you told your daughter you stopped menstruating, I couldn't imagine it. I've never even told anyone I *started*."

The women around the table burst into spontaneous applause. "That was the best thing I ever heard!" cried Carol, laughing helplessly. "What an admission." She wiped her eyes with a napkin. "I've been like that too. I think a lot of women feel the same way."

The women were having fun recalling their menstrual

agonies. It felt as though a dam had broken at the table and previously unspoken feelings were pouring out without shame. Each story tapped into a whole range of emotions around the table. I watched their faces, open, honest, full of feeling, expressing both the humor and the pathos of those years.

"Now we've come around again," I said finally. "Another hurdle to cross. Another life embarrassment. Menopause.

"Let's look at why we're embarrassed. First there's the physical aspect. Not every women has a big problem with hot flashes, but they often occur without warning. You can be standing at a party and suddenly be drenched in sweat. I appear on television sometimes, and my worst nightmare is that I will be sitting on 'Oprah Winfrey,' in front of forty million viewers, and have a hot flash. There's also the insecurity about menstruation. It gets irregular, and you never know when you might have a period. You worry that it might just start and you won't be ready for it and be caught in an embarrassing situation.

"Then there are the changes in your equilibrium and sense of well-being. You might be moody or feel depressed or have less energy. You might feel that you don't have as much control over your emotions as usual, and this can be terrifying. Most women are embarrassed to admit that they feel out of control. We've been conditioned to be stoical about our feelings, and it rarely occurs to people that there might be hormonal reasons for the way they feel, as well as hormonal treatments. What makes menopause even more difficult is that, while you're going through all of these very real changes, you are also being confronted by the negative myths about losing your sexual attractiveness or 'drying up' sexually. No wonder women avoid talking about it."

I paused and looked around the table. They were listening intently—eagerly. This was the first time any of them had been involved in such a discussion—of that I was very sure.

"Earlier we were talking about our embarrassing experiences with menstruation," I went on. "And we were laughing at ourselves a little because we realized that our embarrassment was unfounded. Women menstruate. It's a fact of life. It's normal. Well, the same is true of menopause. It's normal. It's a rite of passage that brings with it some physical changes that we don't especially enjoy but that should not be a source of humiliation. I know that people in our society are a long way from throwing parties when women reach menopause, but we, as women, can take the first step by talking with one another about it."

"I think the support is important, but that's not the only thing we can gain by talking to one another," Naomi said. "Speaking for myself, I want information too. I feel completely ignorant about what to expect."

"For me, it's been so erratic," said Carol. "I'll have a period that lasts two days, then I won't have one, then I'll have one. I thought I would know . . ."

"The onset of menopause is experienced in different ways by different women," I reminded them. "And since the mean age range for menopause is fifty-one to fifty-five, it's unusual for everyone in a group like this to have experienced it. The symptoms themselves are not necessarily cut-and-dried. It took me a while to realize that the strange symptoms I was feeling were the beginnings of menopause. Doctors aren't necessarily very helpful. They don't always take time to explain things fully, and male doctors, of course, have no experience of their own from which to evaluate what's happening."

"Yeah, like what exactly is a hot flash?" asked Naomi. "I don't think I've ever had one, but I'd like to know what to expect."

"Some women experience hardly any symptoms," I said, "although researchers say that almost all menopausal women experience them to some extent. You might feel warm in situations when others are comfortable or experience a sudden feeling of overheating and sweating. Some women report sweating a lot at night. The hot flash is somewhat notorious as the main sign of menopause, but it's not a problem for all women. The hardest part is not knowing and fearing that you might have a sudden hot flash that will embarrass you in front of other people."

"I read somewhere that if you start estrogen replacement therapy (ERT) you won't have hot flashes," said Joyce. "One book said that if you put women on estrogen for a couple of years during the time they would be having hot flashes, they'll be able to get past them."

"Most experts say that ERT will only delay the onset of menopause," I said. "You'll have hot flashes and other symptoms when you're taken off the estrogen. Estrogen replacement therapy is a controversial issue, and the absence of available information makes it hard to weigh the pluses and minuses. Finally it's a decision that is between a woman and her doctor."

"What are the pluses and minuses?" asked Joyce. "I feel so ignorant about it."

"I can give you a broad idea," I said. "On the plus side, estrogen replacement is believed to lower the risk of heart disease and osteoporosis. It also may add elasticity and moisture to the skin, as well as lubricating the vagina. Estrogen can ease the severity of other menopausal symptoms, such as sleep disturbances and mood swings.

"On the minus side, it may increase the incidence of endometrial cancer—cancer of the uterine lining—or breast cancer for some women. There may be other minuses as well, such as an increased risk of gallbladder disease. I don't think they're studied nearly enough. For instance, we don't know what the long-term implications are when you 'fight Mother Nature.'"

"I recently read a great piece in *Lear's* [a magazine for women over forty]," offered Carol. "The woman researched all the alternative medicines, looking for a more natural solution. She ended up choosing a combination of a low dose of hormones, supplemented by the Chinese herb *dong quai*, along with vitamin E and pantothenic acid, which is available in health-food stores. Although I'm not equipped to evaluate her method medically, I was impressed that she reached a happy medium between drugs and natural treatments. I liked the way she took some initiative."

"Yes," I said, "and besides the remedies you mentioned,

there are a few other specific dietary recommendations that can help relieve menopausal symptoms. Caffeine, alcohol, spicy foods, sweets, hot drinks, and large or hot meals are all known to trigger hot flashes. As the article mentioned, vitamin E is often recommended to reduce both the number and severity of hot flashes. To combat the irritability and depression that are present for some women, a 50-mg. vitamin B complex daily may be helpful. Herbal teas, too, have been shown to relieve menopausal symptoms. Some, such as ginseng, red raspberry, licorice, passion flower, and black cohosh, contain estrogen-like properties. And, as a rule, menopausal women should consume 1,500 mg. of calcium each day, either through a regular diet of low-fat dairy products or by taking calcium supplements. That article in *Lear's* is a good example of women sharing their discoveries and know-how with other women—just as we're doing now. When we have information, and when we share our experiences, we gain more power over our bodies. It's like we were saying with menstruation. Much of the problem has to do with not having the reinforcement that this is normal, that it's not something bad happening."

"I've mostly felt symptoms of menopause at night," said June. "I'll get a quivering in my legs and feel restless. I tried taking Valium, but that was no help. It made me feel tired all the time. A friend of mine suggested exercising, so lately I've started walking and getting fresh air in the evening, and that has helped me some."

"When I started having hot flashes, I nearly panicked," admitted Carol, "because they made me feel so out of control. So I decided to take control. I started to keep a record of when they happened and what seemed to trigger them. I found that they seemed to be connected to times I was feeling stress, so I've made changes there. I've started taking yoga, and I'm off caffeinated coffee—that kind of thing. I also dress in layers when I go out, so I can remove clothes if I start feeling hot. Cottons seem more comfortable than polyester.

"The other thing I did was find a new gynecologist who would be more responsive. I contacted the National Women's

Health Network in Washington, D.C. They have a list of women's resources in different parts of the country that will help find caring health professionals, among other things."

"That's useful," I said. "I think at menopause it is appropriate for women to reevaluate their gynecologists to see if they're able to answer the special concerns of this time."

"What about mammograms?" asked June. "Has everyone had a mammogram?" The others in the room nodded, and June cringed. "I'm embarrassed to say that I haven't. I've kept putting it off, and I guess I'd better get moving. But at least I've been manually checking my breasts every month for years now, which I know a lot of women don't do." She sighed. "There seem to be so many things to think about, and a lot of the time I feel so much grumpier. Sometimes I just wish it would all be over."

"I know what you mean," said Marilyn. "I felt the same way when I started going through menopause. I blamed myself and thought that something was wrong with me psychologically. I was going through my divorce then, so I thought that was the reason I was so upset. My friend was the one who suggested that there might be more going on than just my emotions. I went to a doctor who suggested estrogen replacement therapy, and it was like a burden had been lifted to find that there was a physical basis for my depression. It wasn't my fault! Things have smoothed out since then. But I agree with you that a lot of women don't even think about menopause, much less talk to one another about it. I wanted to feel good about menopause, to really experience it as a positive time. But it was tough for me because my ex-husband was having a new baby with his second wife right at the time I started. I felt so angry because I have only one child and at one point I had really wanted to have another baby, but he never did. The timing of his having a baby with his new wife just as I reached the point when I could no longer have children was very hard for me. I felt used up."

"I've never felt depressed," said Joyce, "and it might be because I've changed my health habits a lot. I now exercise at least three times a week, which I've heard is a good way to keep the estrogen that you do have circulating better. It also helps prevent osteoporosis. And I eat better. It is hard to make these changes at this point in my life, but I feel it's worth it if it's going to help me stay on top of things. Sometimes I wonder if this depression thing is just a myth people have about menopause—another way to take away our power." She looked at me. "Karen?"

"Well, I don't like to use the word *depressed*," I agreed. "To some extent you're right that there are myths about menopause that rob women of their self-esteem. But it is also true that hormonal changes affect our emotions. What many feminist experts object to is the prevailing attitude in the medical community that menopause should be treated as a disease. I've heard it suggested that it is a conspiracy between the medical community and the pharmaceutical companies, and if you look at the advertisements for drugs to treat menopause you have to wonder if there is some truth to this. In the ads menopausal women are shown to be drained of energy, moody, wrinkled, and sexually empty—factors that can, they suggest, be reversed with drugs. The message is clearly designed to make women feel, once again, that they are victims of their bodies."

"It's patronizing," said Joyce. "It's like they're saying 'Yes, we understand why you're so depressed. You can't help yourself, poor old cripple.'" Everyone laughed, and Joyce made a face. "I'm not a poor old cripple."

"When my ex-husband's new wife got pregnant, it was painful for me, but I understand why I was feeling that way," added Marilyn. "It was envy, I guess. But most of the time I don't feel bad about myself. Maybe if I had been able to talk about it with someone, it would have been easier."

"Yes, often menopause becomes a burden that women bear alone instead of a joyful transition to the next stage of life," I said quietly. "We can all acknowledge Marilyn's pain because we've felt it ourselves in one way or another. But we wouldn't dream of sharing our feelings—and I think it took a great deal of courage for Marilyn to express what she did. I've found that very few women talk about menopause with their friends or their husbands. And it doesn't occur to most of us to discuss it with our mothers or with other female relatives who have already gone through it."

Joyce laughed. "Oh, forget it. We come from the dark ages of sexual information. Today kids who are ten and twelve know more about sex than I knew when I was twenty. I'm like Carol. My mother never told me about getting my period, so it was pretty traumatic when it started. I thought I was dying."

"Right. And babies were born through your navel." Carol giggled.

"I've been a little better off," said June. "My older sister told me a little bit about menopause. She said it would happen in my early fifties and it wouldn't be so bad. She also told me that having an easy time with menopause runs in the family, so that eased my concerns somewhat. She also explained to me about estrogen. I thought if I took estrogen I would keep having periods forever, and the idea upset me. Imagine—an eighty-year-old woman buying tampons. There seemed something unnatural about putting off menopause forever. But she explained that, because estrogen is combined with progesterone, your flow is diminished."

"Even though menopause has so many negative connotations, there are some positive things too," I said. "Some women talk about feeling a new freedom sexually."

"That's been true for me," agreed Naomi. "There's a new luxury that wasn't there before. That might also have to do with the kids being out of the house. There's so much more privacy now."

"I'm not sure it makes that much difference." June shrugged. "It's nice not to have to think about birth control, but I certainly don't consider it this big sexual time, either."

"I know a woman who is fifty-three, and she missed two periods and was completely devastated—she thought she was pregnant!" said Naomi. "When she found out it was menopause, she was so relieved that she ended up loving the fact that she was going through it."

Affirming the Change of Life

We all smiled at each other in appreciation of what it was like to worry about being pregnant. "You know," I said, "there seems to be more to it than just no longer worrying about pregnancy. It's deeper—more related to our identity. Before menopause a large part of a woman's identity is wrapped up in being a childbearer, a mother. Sometimes women feel empty when they know the potential for motherhood is no longer there. It's important to be aware of these feelings. One woman I interviewed talked about how she longed to give birth just one more time as she approached menopause. Knowing that wasn't practical, she channeled her birthing impulse into writing a book. Ironically, it took nine months to complete. She then 'delivered' it to her editor and felt gratified and fulfilled.

"It's good to find creative ways to cope with a longing that is very common at this stage of life. It's also a time to rethink our sexuality. This is true even for women who don't have children. Our sexual activity always carries the potential for motherhood. When motherhood is no longer a natural part of our sexuality, it changes who we are as sexual beings."

"Sounds good," said Joyce, nodding. "But nobody thinks it's very sexy to grow old. I mean, I still feel the same way I felt ten years ago, and there isn't much difference in my sex life. No brilliant new rebirth of sexiness. Am I missing out on something?"

I laughed. "I didn't mean to imply that women have better sexual experiences after menopause. That's all we need—another standard to try to live up to. I think some women are surprised to find that their sexual responsiveness doesn't really change at all after their childbearing years have ended."

"Don't forget that it isn't just up to us," June added. "The men are there too. Sometimes I think my husband is going through a change of life. They don't have a name for it, but it's real."

"I agree," said Marilyn. "Look at my ex-husband. He married a younger woman, and he's having a baby. He's almost sixty years old."

It was getting late. We had been talking for almost three hours and had finished several pots of decaffeinated coffee. The waiter was hovering.

"I wish we didn't have to stop talking," said Naomi. "This has been great."

"It's the first time I've ever thought of my age in a positive way," said June. "When you talked about celebrating menopause, it blew my mind. It never occurred to me that there might be something good about this."

"I have felt good about my business and what's happening in my life, but I never put it into words before," said Carol. "I see now that we don't share our experiences enough. It's too bad."

"Right," agreed Marilyn. "It's like there's a conspiracy of silence. Nobody wants us to find out how much power we have. They want us to grow into sweet little old ladies like our mothers were and not rock the boat."

"Just rock the chair," Joyce said with a laugh. "Which is ridiculous. I plan to be around until I'm eighty or ninety. I'm not ready to be written off yet."

❋ ❋

It occurred to me later that this was the first time I had participated in a heart-to-heart conversation about menopause. And, although the women in Minneapolis certainly made a valiant effort to speak openly about it, there was a feeling of embarrassment in the air. These women knew remarkably little about this critical turning point in their lives. And yet, by sharing they learned from each other.

Menopause is a muddled time for most of us. Contrary to popular belief, it is not clear when menopause begins; its onset may occur over a period of months or even years. But whenever it starts, we don't exactly feel compelled to announce it to the world. The word itself has an ugly ring. It instantly calls to mind a slew of negatives: loss of sexual appeal or "drying up," hot flashes and other agonies, depression and loss of mental equilibrium. The "change of life" is, in the eyes of the world—and often in our own hearts—a change for the worse.

Even many doctors have difficulty expressing the positive aspects of menopause or communicating that it is a normal transition. My own doctor seemed embarrassed when he confirmed that I was in menopause; he managed to make his diagnosis without uttering the word itself. The brief thrill of excitement I first experienced when I learned I was in the middle of this big change dissipated as my doctor talked soberly about getting rid of something that sounded like a disease.

As I thought more about it, I realized that the experience with my gynecologist told me a great deal about why women are so confused, discouraged, and embarrassed by the onset of menopause. My doctor meant well, perhaps, but in offering a "cure" in lieu of an explanation he had treated me in a condescending manner. He had also managed to communicate to me, with his whispered assurances and pitying smile, that menopause was an unfortunate consequence of aging rather than a special and, in many ways, exciting turn of life. Perhaps a woman doctor might have treated the issue more directly, but even she would not necessarily have congratulated or encouraged me. Doctors, after all, are humanly susceptible to the prevailing attitudes about menopause, and they are no better at facing down the grim reaper than anyone else.

In spite of this feedback I felt compelled by an urge to figure out for myself and for other women what it would mean to really live this time. It was a transition of great significance, a transition I would live only once. Why not make my peace with it? But my friends continued to look at me with horror when I wanted to talk about it, a response that my studies have shown is not unusual.

According to Melody Anderson, co-founder and director of Resources for Midlife and Older Women, there is a tendency in our society to treat the normal process of aging as an illness. "If we compare society's response to the problems of mid-life to those of adolescence," Anderson notes, "we see that the goal is to help teenagers adjust, not to cure them of a pathological condition. The myth attributing women's mid-life problems only to menopause and empty nest syndrome arises from a sexist focus on the reproductive function as the central element in women's lives."

Thinking about Anderson's words, imagine what it would be like if, in the wake of some huge cultural shift, we woke up to find that everyone believed menopause to be a moment of pride in a woman's life, giving it a higher status than the start of menstruation because so much wisdom has been accumulated. How many women throughout the ages have spoken proudly of their daughters reaching womanhood? And even though many young girls would have trouble agreeing that this is such a wonderful thing, the official view is that the start of menstruation is an exciting, transformational event. This change sets in motion the whole range of changes that identify a woman's sexuality. We all know that it is about much more than the ability to bear children. Menstruation is a powerful symbol of the many things it means to be a woman.

Given the power of this symbol, it is probably not surprising that we have such an aversion to the end of the menstrual phase. If the start of menstruation symbolizes the entry into womanhood, what meaning can we give to its ending? Is it then the *end* of womanhood? This deep-seated, usually unspoken fear drives menopausal women into hiding. They lie about their age. They refuse to acknowledge the changes that are happening in their bodies. They fear the judgment of the world that tells them they are no longer sexual.

The idea that women going through menopause are irritable, crazy, and depressed has many of us walking around as though on eggshells, guarding against any tendency to sound overly emotional or irrational. We recoil in horror if there is even a hint in the air that others excuse our behavior with the sympathetic thought that "she's going through the change." To protect ourselves from this shame we watch what we say and fight to keep our demeanors still and sane.

Our attitudes about menopause are culturally driven, and

most of us go along with the prevailing story. But when women are asked to share how they *really* feel, the story is often quite different from the gloomy picture we are accustomed to seeing. Last year Sonja McKinlay, a psychologist who is president of the New England Research Institute in Watertown, Massachusetts, published the results of a five-year study she had conducted with twenty-three hundred menopausal women. McKinlay found that most of the study's participants expressed relief that they no longer had to be concerned about pregnancy, contraception, and menstruation. And although 70 percent of the women initially expressed regret about menopause, four-and-a-half years later *only three women* still expressed regret. Furthermore a vast majority of the women (85 percent) reported that they were never depressed, and most of the women who did report depression said they were depressed before the onset of menopause. The researchers suggested that the stereotype of the depressed, cranky menopausal woman might have evolved because doctors tended to see those women more than women who weren't experiencing any problems. The same might be true of the much-talked-about "empty nest syndrome." Women who don't experience depression when their children leave home are less likely to talk about it or seek professional help.

In 1989 *Lear's* published the results of a survey it commissioned from Lou Harris Associates of educated women between the ages of forty and sixty-five. The magazine reported: "Women of this age perceive themselves to be, and *are*, unusually vital, productive, spirited, sexy, loving, and in the thick of personal and cultural change. An astonishing 59 percent of the women we surveyed say that the best years of their lives are now.... Of the 700 college-educated women we polled nationwide ... the great majority believe they are richer, stronger, more accomplished, more serene, and happier than they have ever been."

Studies like those conducted by McKinlay and *Lear's* go a long way toward collapsing the myth of the miserable and fragile menopausal woman. It is a positive sign that magazines like *Lear's* even exist, speaking freely and without embarrassment about the issues encountered at the change of life. But such examples are limited and, judging by the feedback I received from women, not very accessible.

Women themselves can be the catalysts for change, even in small ways. For example, the women in the Minneapolis group spoke of their confusion about the physical and psychological manifestations of menopause, and they did not know where they could find credible answers to their questions. All admitted to feeling intimidated by the prospect of discussing the matter with their gynecologists—but why? Sometimes you have to be the one to initiate the dialogue with your gynecologist: go prepared with specific questions. Here is a list of sample questions. Don't wait to ask them until you are already experiencing menopausal symptoms. If you understand in advance of menopause what to expect, you will feel that you have greater control over your body as it goes through this normal life change.

Your gynecologist will also be better able to help you if you arrive equipped with some specific information about your family history. Heredity plays a critical role in determining your susceptibility to age-related health problems, such as osteoporosis (thinning of the bones) and cervical and breast cancers.

QUESTIONS FOR THE GYNECOLOGIST

1. How do I know I am approaching menopause? What are the early signs? Are they the same for every woman? If not, how do they differ?

2. What is a mammogram? When and how often should I have one? What happens during a mammogram?

3. What are hot flashes? Does every woman get them? How long do they last? Can they be controlled?

4. Will menopause affect me psychologically? Will I become depressed or experience mood swings? If so, how can I reduce the psychological problems?

5. Will menopause affect my sexual life? Will my interest in sex change? Will I experience vaginal dryness or other symptoms? If this happens, is there a way to reverse it or ease the discomfort?

6. Can I still become pregnant at any point during menopause? At what point can I be sure that pregnancy is no longer possible?

7. Do menopausal women have special nutritional needs? Can some of the symptoms of menopause be handled nutritionally?

8. What is osteoporosis? How do I know if I am at risk for developing it? What can I do to prevent it?

9. What is estrogen therapy? What are the benefits of taking estrogen? What are the dangers? What are the specific effects of estrogen? For example, will it delay menopause? Will I avoid having hot flashes or other symptoms if I take estrogen? Will I continue to have periods?

10. What are the medical conditions that are most common for menopausal women? How do I know if I am at risk for cancers or other diseases? What are the signs I should watch for? How often should I be examined by a physician?

Another way you can take charge of your menopausal period is by keeping records and monitoring what is happening to you. Ann Voda's excellent booklet *Menopause, Me and You* includes specific instructions and charts for recording and evaluating ovulation and symptoms such as hot flashes. You can order this pamphlet by writing to Ann M. Voda, Ph.D., 1325 G Street N.W., Washington, D.C. 20005.

Another good service is the Resources for Midlife and Older Women, located at 226 E. 70th Street, Suite 1-C, New York, New York 10021; 212-439-1913. The staff and volunteers provide resource and referral services, directing women to programs that can help with specific problems. They also offer individual counseling and support groups.

—3—
A Time of Achievement

Most of us are taught from our earliest years to place limits on our precious gift of life. We are led to believe that life offers only one chance. The question "What are you going to be when you grow up?" means "What *one thing* are you going to do when you grow up?" We are trapped by this notion so that, as we grow older, we become paralyzed by fear. Living a successful life becomes reduced to achieving prominence in one field by the time we are forty or fifty. Talking to women my age, I have heard over and over the fearful refrains:

"What can I do now? I've been a mother all my life, and I don't know how to do anything else."

"It's too late for me to learn anything new."

"I've always had a dream, but maybe I'm too old to try it now."

"I made a choice when I was twenty, and now I'm stuck with it."

We believe what we are taught to believe, that there's an invisible wall we hit sometime in our mid-forties. Even though we may have thirty or more years of active living left, the wall stops us dead in our tracks and imprisons us in the choices of our past. In the process, we allow ourselves to be defined by our previous successes or failures or to limit our options with a self-deprecating shrug: "I am just a housewife . . . I am just a mother . . . I am just . . ."

Jenny, fifty, added a new perspective to this common dilemma of how to move beyond this perceived wall. Jenny was a teacher who was trying to decide whether or not to make a change.

"I almost have to say this in a whisper," she admitted, blushing. "I'm not sure anyone would understand. I've been a teacher all my life, but I've always felt like the real me was a writer. It's as though I'm a writer inside a teacher."

It was a provocative thought. Many people, I have found, go along in life on their chosen path, secretly believing that their "real" selves lie elsewhere. I began to ask women to think about this and discovered that many secret selves lie buried. "I am a psychic inside a secretary," one woman told me. "I am a teacher inside a mother," another said. "I am a social worker inside a businesswoman." "I am a politician inside a psychologist." "I am an artist inside an editor."

Nearly everyone, if prodded, could name an inner self far different from her outer self. I decided to explore this idea further, to find out how it could increase our understanding of what we dream of and what is possible in our lives.

Over lunch one day in Westchester, New York, three women, including Jenny, began to explore this concept with me.

"Within all of us there is another self—perhaps our true self," I said. "It seems to me that this other self manifests itself in our dreams about whom we might become and what we might do at a later point in life."

"Yes," Jenny agreed. "I didn't give up the idea of becoming a writer completely when I became a teacher. I just put it on hold. The nice thing about writing is that you can do it anytime, no matter how old you are. I read recently that Cynthia Freeman, who wrote several big bestsellers, didn't start writing until she turned fifty, and there seem to be a lot of examples of this."

"So, will you now stop teaching and become a writer?" Leslie, a psychologist of fifty, asked.

"I'm not sure whether I'll do it now or after I retire," Jenny said. "I have no idea if I have the ability. I haven't written anything in thirty years."

Leslie frowned thoughtfully. "I guess what I'm getting at is the sense that, even though we have these secret dreams of doing other things that we think are more true to our natures, we keep putting off doing them. They're like fantasies that we can take out and think about, but we don't really believe they're real. I have a pretty successful career, and I enjoy it. But I've always been fascinated with politics and have been active in my community. The question is: what kind of risk would it entail for me to get more involved? And I have to consider the possibility that I really may be too old."

Leslie, who is a tall, attractive blond with an intelligent, lively face, didn't appear too old for anything.

"You're not too old," I said. "Public service is an ageless profession. However, the question of risk is valid. The more comfortable we become with the status quo, the harder it is to make changes. But I also think that having an all-or-nothing attitude can trap us. We don't necessarily need to make grand, dramatic choices, like 'I'm going to stop being a teacher and go for broke as a writer.' Usually there's a middle ground where both are possible. For example, I worked as a psychiatric nurse in a suicide prevention center where I could do counseling before I started preparing to enter private practice as a psychotherapist.

"Another thing to keep in mind is that sometimes we hold ourselves back because we are afraid we won't be able to accept what we find," I said. "If you've always had a dream and said to yourself, 'When I do this or that—that's when my life will become satisfying,' or 'That's when I'll really be me,' there is some danger of being torn apart if the reality does not match the dream. Especially when we invest so much in the dream. Jenny, you've made the idea of writing more than just something you'd like to do someday. You've made it a part of your identity. However, I think you have to be cautious about what you call your identity, because it's not a static thing. Our identities grow and change; they're different at different points in our lives. So maybe the things you believed about yourself twenty years ago are no longer true."

"Interesting," said Paula, forty-eight, a New York publishing executive. "That makes me think of a woman I met recently through a friend. She's in her mid-sixties, and she was very much the housewife and mother until she was fifty. She got married right out of high school, after World War II, and she never even considered doing anything else. At least that's what she says, but I think she must have had some dreams that she kept private. So, when she was fifty, she went out and got a job as a secretary, and she started taking night classes at the community college. Her family was shocked. They didn't know this woman who was suddenly such a whirlwind of activity. It took them a while to get used to it, but now everyone has a completely different idea of what her identity is. When I met her, it occurred to me how we make demands on people not to change. When they change, it threatens us, because we have to learn to relate to them in new ways."

"That's a good observation," I said. "I think that's why it's so hard to make changes and follow dreams that are outside our usual roles. But as your friend demonstrated, it is possible, even though it sometimes takes time for people to adjust. In fact, for many women this period becomes a time when they feel freer to pursue their own course of action, unhampered by the expectations of others. Isak Dinesen might have been referring to this when she wrote, 'Women, when they are old enough to have done with the business of being women, and can let loose their strength, must be the most powerful creatures in the world.' In other words, when you're done with doing what's expected of you, you can tap into the incredible power of being yourself."

"That's an interesting sentiment," said Paula, "considering that, in our culture, age is associated with a lessening of power rather than with greater power."

"Especially for women," added Leslie. "But in one sense I can see her point. I've noticed in myself a tendency in the last few years to worry less about what other people think of me, and it has made me stronger and, I believe, more effective. For women it has never been possible, or at least it has been very difficult, to separate ourselves from whom we are expected to be as women. Even as we pursue careers, there's always a pull back and forth, between our place at work and our place at home. I feel less torn now simply because I no longer have a day-to-day role in my children's lives. I have more freedom and, therefore, can pay more attention to myself."

"I agree with Leslie," said Paula, "but since I didn't get married and have children, it's been somewhat different for me. When I was young, I always expected to get married, and I almost did once. But things never worked out, and time went on." She smiled wistfully. "Even though I wasn't married, for a long time—well into my thirties—it was my main focus, more important than my career. I used to worry a lot that my slightly untraditional style was getting in the way. I tried to make concessions to the norm, but they never lasted long. But when I reached my forties, I noticed a gradual change, more of an acceptance of myself. I stopped feeling that there was something wrong with me, and at that point, I know, I became stronger. What I'm trying to say is that it doesn't matter whether a woman is married or single; she is still preoccupied in youth with thoughts about marriage and family, because that's what's expected of her by others."

"Let's consider Dinesen's comment from another angle," I suggested. "All of us here have reached the same stage in our lives. It's too late to go back and relive our youth. What I found interesting about this idea of achieving greater strength with age was, one, that it is in direct opposition to the way our society normally views the mature woman and, two, that we in this room are living examples of what Dinesen is saying. Speaking for myself, when I was younger I always had the feeling that there was plenty of time for me to make whatever mark I was going to make. I could fantasize about things I wanted to try, without taking the risk. But there's more urgency now. The future has closed in. I'm sure we all experience this in one way or another. Jenny, take you. You've always had a picture of the future in which you were a writer. Are you beginning to feel that the future is now?"

Jenny considered this for a moment. "I have found it more on my mind," she said finally. "But I haven't done anything about it, and I'm not sure why. It wouldn't be any big thing for me to take a writing class or start putting things down on paper. Maybe I'm afraid I'll find out I'm not good enough to do it for a living."

"Can I say something?" Paula waved a hand in the air. "Maybe you have to separate your love for writing and your will to write from your fear of judgment. If a person who loves writing doesn't write because her writing is not accepted by others as being 'good,' however that is determined, that doesn't necessarily mean she isn't a writer."

"Maybe . . . but what good is writing if no one reads it?"

"My point," pressed Paula, "is that you should evaluate what success or failure might mean to you. I know a seventy-year-old woman who has been writing poetry all her life. Every week she hosts a poetry reading in her home. Sometimes she'll sell a poem, but there's not much money in it, and the point is, she gets a great deal of pleasure out of writing poetry and talking to other poets. Her definition of success is quite different from the one another writer might have."

"That's a good point," said Leslie enthusiastically. "It could apply to me too. I always thought if I got involved in politics it would have to mean running for an office someday, which is a great risk and very expensive. Maybe I've been thinking too narrowly. There are many different ways of being involved in politics, and not all of them involve an equal amount of risk. I can take things slowly at first until I see how deeply I want to get involved."

"We hear the concept frequently expressed in the media that we should be 'true' to ourselves," I observed. "And we probably worry too much about what that means. After all, there are always things in life that we wish for but never have. We make one choice, and it cancels out another. Perhaps the key is to remain open to the possibility that we can fulfill certain dreams without feeling guilty about choosing not to fulfill them. Jenny, the feeling that there's a writer inside you shouldn't be a terrible burden or something you have to prove to yourself. It's more like a desire or a dream you have. It could open up a new adventure if you try it, but you might decide that you have other priorities that are more meaningful."

"I like the idea that I have choices I can still make," said Jenny. "I don't want to be a person who feels stuck. And I'm delighted to be discovering now that being fifty isn't the closed door I once thought it would be. In fact—" she pulled herself up straight and smiled at us across the table—"I feel positively young right now."

In every conversation I had with women on the subject of pursuing their dreams, switching careers, or just doing something they'd always wanted to do, age was inevitably raised as a perceived barrier. And while everyone could readily name examples of women who had pursued new directions when they were in their fifties and sixties (Lillian Carter, who joined the Peace Corps when she was sixty-five, was often mentioned, as was Mother Theresa), there was a consensus that these were rare examples, outside the realm of the average woman. Some people expressed the view that the publicity surrounding the achievements of older women was somewhat condescending. "I am tired of hearing all the hype about how age doesn't make any difference and how we can do anything we want," said one woman almost angrily. "That attitude covers up the real truth, which is that there is tremendous prejudice against older women and that the outstanding examples that do exist are the exception rather than the rule."

Maybe so. But another way of looking at it is that they are the role models—the heroines, if you will—of a new movement. The avant-garde. Fundamental changes in our cultural understanding do not occur of their own accord. In fact public attitudes often lag behind the reality, and age is one arena where this is particularly evident. Why else would so many people feel compelled to lie about their age?

It is easy for women to feel intimidated by the perception that our opportunities in the workplace decline as we reach the middle years. A recent report released by the National Commission on Working Women, called "Women, Work and Age: A Report on Older Women and Employment," holds both good and bad news for the female work force. On one hand it reported that, although 54 percent of mid-life and older women are in the United States work force, they have failed, on the whole, to break into the higher-paying male-dominated jobs. It is suggested that this has resulted from the many social constraints and "legal" forms of discrimination that existed during their earlier years. As a group older women earn less than younger women and all ages of men. In 1985 women aged forty-five to fifty-four working full-time earned an average of $17,009 a year; men of the same age group averaged $29,880. "Although women have access to training and 'ports of entry' within female-dominated fields," the report said, "the ladders either dead-end just beyond the entry level or don't exist at all." There is something of a catch-22 for women in the workplace. Since employers are often reluctant to invest in younger women who might leave them to have children, the mature women whose children are grown have not had a chance to build the history of advancement, and they are stopped short in their career tracks.

On the other hand, the report noted: "Despite the culturally-based myths about older women, in some respects older women outshine younger workers. They are less likely to leave the labor force or change jobs—the turnover rate for women in their 50s was one-sixth that of women in their 20s in one study. ... Older women workers also have lower absenteeism rates and fewer work-related accidents."

The term *displaced homemaker* is a familiar part of the job lingo, and statistics indicate that many of these workers are older women. According to one study conducted in the late 1970s, of the more than one million persons who reported themselves discouraged in their efforts to find work, one-third were over fifty-five and one-half were over forty, with women comprising the greater proportion of both groups.

Having said that, it is also of course true that some professions seem less locked into youth than others. I suspect that my patients have confidence in me because I have so many years of experience. Television may treat me less kindly as I grow older, but my work in one-on-one therapy seems to be enhanced by my age.

It was at the point when I was considering the question of which professions were most acceptable for mature women that I met Arlene, a fifty-year-old black model who did not fit any of my preconceived categories.

I met Arlene, a glamorous woman, in a glamorous setting, a party for *Lear's* magazine. During the course of the evening we found ourselves seated together and began to talk.

"I tried to get into modeling a couple years ago," I told her. "It's wasn't right for me, but I'm fascinated by the idea of a fifty-year-old woman taking on a profession that is usually associated with youth."

"I've never worried much about age," Arlene admitted. "Part of that is because black people tend to look younger longer because of our pigmentation. But more importantly, the age issue seems superficial because we have so many other issues to deal with. Ageism is the lowest thing on my list of concerns, which include racism and sexism."

"I see your point," I said. "Nevertheless, since you've chosen modeling as a profession, you must be aware of striking back at the ageist stereotypes."

"Yes," she agreed, "I've thought about that. But there are other things I'd like to do besides being a model, so I don't worry about reaching a point when I can no longer model. I want to make a lasting contribution to the next generation. Maybe that means working with kids—I'm not sure. But I do see that we are living in a world preoccupied by self; people don't seem to care about each other anymore. I would hate for that to be the lasting legacy of our generation, so I'll do what I can to change it."

In the course of our conversation I described my recent struggle with making a change in my work. At a point in my career when I thought that the future was secure, my radio program on WOR in New York City was canceled, and I was suddenly out of a job. The experience made me feel vulnerable and intensely aware of my age. For a while I wondered if I would be able to find work that was satisfying. It took me several agonizing months of indecision before I decided on a course—to leave radio and rebuild my psychotherapy practice. It turned out to be a very good decision. But remembering my own feelings at that time, I asked Arlene if she had any fears about taking risks at her age.

"Oh, sure. As I get older, I have moments of feeling a great need for caution." Then Arlene smiled and her dark eyes danced. "But more often I just throw caution to the wind. I ask you: what is there to lose at this point?"

So, I found, although ageism does exist, women like Arlene have demonstrated that it is possible to overcome it. And the more I explored the subject, the more convinced I became that the ten-year period between forty-five and fifty-five is a time of empowerment. That fact was demonstrated amply by the women I met, who were talking about it and experiencing it.

Nevertheless there is a perception that the process of growth and learning becomes more difficult as we get older. It may be that this perception stems from our deep belief that there are those who know and those who don't know and that we ourselves always fall into the latter category rather than the former. By the time we reach adulthood, we have already judged ourselves, and that judgment only becomes hardened with age. How casually we say "I'm not the kind of person who could ever do that" or "I just don't have the head for it." Or, as I did, when I refused for several years to use a computer, "Technical things are beyond my ability."

And yet I find that women are tentatively testing the waters for a new definition of career and work, and this excites me. It makes sense that women could be the pioneers, because our career experiences are so often much less conventional than those of our male counterparts. We have a greater incentive to search for options that break with tradition, because tradition has not always been kind to us. It is in our hands to re-create our work patterns in less rigid ways that allow us to avoid the paralysis that sets in both with success and with lack of success. We are capable of blossoming in the fluid motion of our work years and of respecting ourselves enough to try new things.

Carolyn Heilbrun, in *Writing a Woman's Life*, offers a tantalizing idea that women can take with them into their middle years. She notes that, for women, "the coming of age portends all the freedoms men have always known and women never—mostly the freedom from fulfilling the needs of others and from being a female impersonator." Her use of the word *impersonator* refers to the idea that in our younger years we mostly serve the feminine ideal, often appearing and behaving as others think we should. But later we have the chance to be more authentically ourselves, and this discovery, if we dare to make it, can transform our future engagements.

DECIDING WHAT TO DO WITH THE REST OF YOUR LIFE

Have you ever had this experience? You drive to a certain place several times with someone else behind the wheel. You believe you know the way, but when you get into the driver's seat you realize that you haven't paid enough attention to the landmarks and turns to get there by yourself. You may find that your life now is a lot like that. Many women have confided to me that, although they feel they are in a perfect position to start different careers, return to school, or take on new projects (often because their children are grown), now that they are free to pilot their own lives they have lost the ability to navigate the course they really want to follow.

How do you reorient yourself to your direction in life? The

best way is to do some research on yourself. Begin by asking yourself the following questions:

1. Looking back, during which period was I most satisfied?
2. Which things did I find so satisfying about this period?
3. What was my favorite place to live?
4. Why was that place my favorite?
5. In the past, which activities (including my hobbies, volunteer work, and work for pay) did I find pleasure and satisfaction in?
6. What have people always told me I'm good at?
7. If I had one month to live, what would I regret never having had a chance to do?
8. What things would I like to be known for in the future?

Often women who ask themselves these questions find themselves saying "I forgot about that," referring to a special talent or activity. It's like Jenny's idea of having another person inside the person you presently project to the world. When you reach back and reconnect with your past, you encounter yourself as a person with many possibilities you may not have known you had. There is no reason you cannot fulfill these now.

For the past year, I have, in my spare moments, become quite involved in creating artistic collages, and in the process I've discovered a deep-seated artistic sensibility that I have begun to bring into other parts of my life. I have also become aware that my artistic interest actually harks back to my childhood, when my family lived in a house far outside town. I was alone a lot, and for entertainment I used to spend hours cutting pictures from Sears catalogs and putting them together into scenes. As anyone who lived during that time will remember, the Sears catalogs were often called "wish books." From these I cut out people, clothing, appliances, furniture—everything I needed to invent stories—and I created collages around these stories.

The collages I have been doing this year are similar; they reflect the underlying themes of my dreams and the sense of who I am at fifty. When my collages were accepted for display by a local art show I felt very proud. And although I did not go on to pursue this artistic direction professionally, I have turned it into a very satisfying hobby that allows me to fulfill a side of myself that had not previously been fulfilled. This experience has reminded me that it is not only the work we get paid for that counts. Hobbies are undervalued in our society, but in reality they can become the most enriching aspects of our lives. So, while you're considering what you will do next, do not forget those things that will simply give you pleasure. While there are sometimes age barriers to employment, there is no age barrier to doing the things you enjoy and sometimes we have to think beyond the restraints of our jobs to get the things we really want out of life.

But even if you know the course you'd like to pursue, you may be feeling that your self-esteem isn't very high right now. If you find yourself thinking that it's too late for you to do anything significant with your life, you need to find a historical role model, a "sister" if you will, to remind you of how powerful you are. For me this is Georgia O'Keeffe. I love the way she was so creative and full of life, even when she was very old. Nothing could stop her. I have one of her paintings hanging above my desk in my office to remind me that I too can be that way. When I think about her, as I do whenever I look at the painting, it is easier for me to imagine how powerful I will be into my later years.

4
Beauty Lost and Found

A forty-eight-year-old woman wrote to me:

"I study my face more often these days, pressing it close to the mirror, wondering how I really look. The process is less objective than it once was; today's reflection is not so easy to evaluate.

"I stand there staring, and long stretches of time pass as I examine every pore and every wrinkle. Sometimes I experiment, wondering how I'd look with the aid of plastic surgery. First I pull my eyes back slightly, smoothing the lines that spread out from them like cracked glass. I open my eyes wide and press downward, observing from between my fingers the way the little pouches disappear. With my forefingers I pull back my cheeks, at the same time pushing my thumbs against my neck to create the tightness of a face-lift. I'm never sure what these experiments show me—if I like the new effects I create or not.

"I am aware of my face all of the time. My powers of observation are as sharp as those of a detective. I notice when I break out into a natural smile my face erupts into hundreds of creases, and I practice keeping my facial muscles perfectly still—especially when I'm in a situation when I want to look younger. Age spots—yes, I'm beginning to see age spots—blossom like freckles, and I take care to mask them with a new brand of makeup.

"All the while I am focusing on my face, I am feeling a series of disturbing emotions. Regret. Frustration. But the predominant emotion is guilt. Why can't I be more accepting of the natural process of growing older? Why does my aging face make me ashamed? Why do I look at myself and think 'the ravages of age' rather than 'the beauty of maturity'?"

I smiled to myself when I read her words, because each one of them rang so true. What woman has not agonized in just these ways or studied her face with such intensity as if to ask, "Mirror, mirror on the wall . . ."?

As we reach our middle years, we grow less secure with the message in the mirror. How substantial is the evidence of our aging? What do others see when they look at us?

Our critical cultural standards do not leave much room for reassurance once we cross the line that separates youth from the rest of our lives. When we were young, no matter what other crises filled our lives, we believed (as we were taught) that as long as we could greet the world with fresh, young faces any dream could be realized. But now we are more insecure because we know that we are being judged by new standards—in our jobs, in our bedrooms, and even on the street.

Of course our concern with physical appearance does not occur as a new factor when we cross the line between youth and maturity. It is simply another facet of an old nemesis that has been with us since the earliest point of our recollections. Being pretty is something we were always conditioned to value, and it's no wonder, since a woman's beauty has been considered the source of her power and her greatness throughout time. "She never yet was foolish that was fair," wrote Shakespeare, and the world agreed. "Was this the face that launched a thousand ships?" asked Christopher Marlowe. And Pascal noted, in a speculation that surely put a powerful historical character in her place: "Cleopatra's nose, had it been shorter, the whole face of the world would have been changed."

Given our obsession with the ideal of female beauty, the results of a Lou Harris Associates poll, that 75 percent of women think about their physical appearance frequently and 99 percent of women would like to change their physical appearance, are not surprising. If beauty and power are synonymous, why not go for the gold?

A friend told me, "When I meet someone for the first time, or even when I am walking down the street among strangers, a curiosity lingers in the back of my mind: How old do I look to them? Do they see me as someone who might be in her thirties? Early forties? Late forties? Fifties? I play coy games with people, saying 'How old do you think I am?' and am furious when they guess my age right or, God forbid, think I'm older. But I also feel insecure when they tell me I look younger, because I assume they're lying. They can't win at this game, and neither can I." I knew what she meant. I can't help feeling happy when people express surprise that I have a twenty-six-year-old son. "You must have had him when you were fifteen," they say as I blush with pleasure.

I was amused when I read this line from a woman writer who was only on the brink of forty: "As a sex object, I am depreciating by the day." I thought, "how true," but then I questioned my own feelings. Surely I have never been interested in being a sex object. Neither have most of the women I've met. Far from it! But it seems that, whether we will it or not, this "body thing" gets under our skins and becomes, if not a major obsession, at least a minor one. As we reach our mature years, we mourn the loss of our youthful skin tone and body resiliency as much as we might mourn the loss of a very dear friend.

The facts are unmistakable, inescapable. Our bodies, as we age, show the passage of time:

Hair loses the color of its youth.
Age spots develop on our faces and hands.
Skin becomes thinner and less resilient.
Breasts sag.
Waistlines grow resistant to exercise and diet.

Lines deepen around our mouths and eyes.

Pouches gather under our eyes.

Neck lines gain prominence.

Tooth problems and gum infections are common.

Eyesight and hearing grow less sharp.

Small, wiry hairs appear on our chins.

    When I was forty-seven, I tried a new look. Maybe I was just tired of the way I had worn my hair for years. Maybe I felt a new hairstyle would make me appear younger. Whatever the reasons, I had my hair cut, permed, and colored with blond highlights. These changes made me feel younger, because my hair had been prematurely gray and it had been a long time since I had seen myself blond. It was quite a jolt to look in the mirror and see this formerly demure woman with what could only be described as *boisterous* hair.

    I knew I looked younger, and I noticed that I drew a lot more looks from men than I had with my previous style. It was fun in the beginning, but it never really felt like me. In retrospect I see that it might have been a last fling with youth and a chance to be the outrageous self I had never before had the nerve to be. Since my husband, Bob, was so enthusiastic about my new look, I kept it longer than I otherwise would have. But I longed for a return to my more conservative style. I even envied my friends who had not changed their gray hair. Finally I went partway back. I returned to my original style, but I kept the blond. Eventually I will let the white hair grow out again, and I will be natural. I'm looking forward to that time.

    I am more aware now of what my personal campaign against my body's aging was designed to achieve. And I think that my effort to go into modeling at the age of forty-seven was more than just the desire to try something I'd always wanted to try. It was also a way of asking the question "Am I still attractive enough that people will want to look at me?" Like many women, I had always equated being attractive with looking young.

I know a woman who, while looking in the mirror, repeats, like a mantra, "You are beautiful... Your lines add character... You look fine." I asked her if it helped, and she said wryly, "It helps me. I really believe it. Now the trick is to convince the men I date."

❋- -❋

As I was developing this book, I sent out a survey to fifty women between the ages of forty-five and fifty-five who agreed to respond to a questionnaire about their feelings toward their bodies. Their responses struck many familiar chords.

Many of the women I interviewed admitted that their husbands had some difficulty accepting the physical aging of their wives. This didn't surprise me, given the strength of the cultural ideal, which for women includes youth. But these women also said it helped to talk about it openly and use the opportunity to discuss the important things about their marriages—such as the "best friends" aspect, the shared memories, and their hopes for the future. In other words, to take the focus off the physical. One fifty-year-old woman, married ten years, said that her husband still takes her out on special dates. He asks her out, tells her generally what to wear, picks her up, and surprises her with a planned evening. "This keeps the romance in our marriage," she observed. "And it helps us overcome some of the anxieties we both feel about looking older."

All of the women acknowledged being very conscious throughout their lives of the special advantages of being physically attractive. "I knew I was smart," said one. "But I also sensed that being smart was not enough. It was a great relief to me that I was also considered pretty, because I knew that being smart and unattractive would be a deadly, and very lonely, combination."

Another recalled her work in the fledgling women's movement of the 1960s. "There were a lot of accusations directed toward women who were feminists. We were often drawn as sad, pathetic women, too unattractive or unfeminine to find men. There was a sense that the entire feminist movement was built on sour grapes. Since we were not attractive ourselves, we would scorn the values of being beautiful. More than once I had men say to me, 'What's a pretty girl like you doing mixed up with these others?' "

A black woman remarked, "When I was young, black was definitely *not* considered beautiful. I was very critical about the way I looked. In those days I could find no examples in magazines or on television of women who looked like me. I learned to accept it, and perhaps it allowed me to focus on other, more important things. But I find it quite ironic that today, when black women are finally coming into their own, I'm past the age when I can feel exhilarated by a sense of beauty. It's not something I dwell on, but I confess to an occasional sense of regret."

Another woman recalled, "I was fiercely independent, very strong, dedicated to my career. I tried to present an image of one for whom looks were unimportant. But I was secretly fixated on the way I looked and took great pains, always in private, to be sure I looked attractive. I was one of those women who rose from bed at the crack of dawn to apply subtle makeup touches—a spot of rouge, a little lip gloss—and then returned to bed so my man would think I was naturally beautiful. I would have been absolutely humiliated had any man caught me in the act of applying makeup at four in the morning. Now, at forty-six, I can laugh at that behavior and evaluate what it meant. I am more conscious now of getting past the superficial."

"I saw the movie *On Golden Pond*, and I envied Jane Fonda in her bikini," recalled one woman. "But when I see her exercising, it seems too frenetic. It appears that you can't be in really great shape unless you're willing to make it a full-time pursuit, and I'm not willing."

A Roman Catholic nun shared a unique perspective. "Because of my looks, when I was in my twenties people would constantly marvel that I had chosen to join a religious order. And I'll admit that I had my vanities. I liked hearing the comments, because they made me feel somehow powerful. It would come as a surprise to many people to realize that even the most dedicated religious women are concerned about their looks. I remember a sixty-year-old sister who lived in my convent during the 1960s, when we began making changes in our garb. She had been in the order for forty-two years, and she had never appeared in public without being completely covered by the protective robes of our order. When those of us who were younger began lobbying for shorter, less restrictive habits, she was one of our most bitter foes. I thought at first that it was a silly moralism on her part. I later found out that she was deeply ashamed of her thick legs. And it occurred to me then that the full religious habits allowed women who were not beautiful to achieve a power and mystery that may not have been available to them in the secular world. This sister, like many others, was rightfully worried about losing that special position."

Since the ideal of physical beauty is established for women from youth, I asked women to talk about when they first became aware of physical changes brought on by maturity—and how they felt about them.

"I was always very aware of my looks," said one. "I used to love going to parties and making an entrance into a room, knowing that men were looking at me. But over the years I got tired of having to be 'on' all the time. Now I'm looking forward to the time when men won't be looking me over. It will be a relief."

Another woman expressed a similar sentiment. "When I turned fifty, I felt relieved that I would no longer need to be so conscious of impressing men."

"I never thought of myself as growing older until my husband had an affair with a woman in her early thirties," said a woman of forty-seven. "He eventually left me and moved in with her. Occasionally I would see them together in town. She had such a slim, youthful body and long brown hair that she swung about in a very appealing way. After seeing them I would go home and stare at my face in the mirror for a long time, and all I could see were the lines. No one could ever convince me that my husband didn't leave me because I was growing older, and I felt betrayed—not by him but by my own body."

Another woman related a story of the day she and her teenage daughter were looking at family picture albums. "She stopped at a picture of me when I was in my mid-twenties, and she said, very surprised, 'Mom, you were so beautiful then.' The word *then* grated on me. It was only at that moment that I saw how much I had changed—that I was no longer young."

Another woman said, "I didn't notice anything too different about the way I looked. But I started to notice that my friends looked older, and then I wondered if they saw me that way too. I wasn't sure if I was seeing things clearly when I looked in the mirror."

"What finally convinced me to stop smoking was that I could see the effects on my face," one woman said. "Those vertical lines above my lip were growing more prominent. It's funny that the health threat didn't scare me away, but the vanity did."

"I am forty-eight years old," said a woman who had always lied about her age. "But my perception of my age has always been off. I matured early, and as a teenager I could pass for twenty. I dated college guys when I was fourteen. Then, when I turned thirty, I felt I looked younger, and I stayed twenty-nine all during my thirties. It started as kind of a joke, but then it just stuck. For the past few years I've said I was in my early forties. I reinvent who I am as I see fit. I lie about my age in order to reduce the negative stereotypes, and I don't feel the least bit guilty about it."

"I went to a video dating service," said a divorced woman. "When I told them I was forty-five, the two young, beautiful women who ran the agency looked like they felt sorry for me—or, at least, that's what I imagined. I turned around and left, because I knew it would be worse if I signed up and no men wanted to meet me because of my age. Suddenly the idea of meeting men that way seemed futile, because there were so many younger women also applying."

The same woman related the following story. "One night I was up late watching an old Elizabeth Taylor movie. In it she played a middle-aged woman whose husband had lost interest in her. She went off to some distant, exotic place—I think it was Switzerland—and had her entire face remade so that she looked like a beautiful young woman. Of course her husband was once again desperately in love with her. I remember fantasizing about going away and having plastic surgery, then moving to a new city where no one knew me and telling everyone I was thirty years old."

In a similar vein another single woman said that she considered taking six years off her age when she met a man. "I'm forty-six, but I know I could pass for forty. The problem is that it gets too complicated. If I take six years off my age, I have to take six years off my daughter's age—either that or say she was born when I was seventeen. It grows too hard to tell lies, because my age is a reflection of everything I've been in my life, and to change it I would have to make up a new me."

About half the women I surveyed admitted that they would like to feel less anxious about looking older. The phrase "growing old gracefully" came up a lot, with women expressing the longing to let age take its course in a comfortable way—and to feel good about the process. These women felt embarrassed about spending a lot of energy on looking younger, as though they were failing to appreciate the natural process of life. But others felt differently. There was a sentiment, expressed by the other half of the women, that they were completely comfortable about taking steps to look younger if they felt those steps were realistic and affordable.

Plastic surgery, once the domain of a special few, has become the woman's common recourse now. Today it is a relatively minor operation to have the pouches removed from beneath one's eyes. Liposuction can reshape the contours of a thickened waistline or bulging hips. Collagen injections nonsurgically fill in facial lines.

How do women feel about having the means to extend the appearance of youth into their older years?

Most of the women I interviewed had not had plastic surgery, but nearly all of them had thought about it. Several women said they were planning to have plastic surgery so they could better compete with their younger colleagues professionally; others considered surgery a way to remain on a level playing field socially.

"Ten years ago I laughed off the idea that I would ever do

anything so 'artificial,' " a forty-nine-year-old woman said. "I viewed plastic surgery as an unconscionable vanity. Now I have mixed feelings. On the one hand I still feel that it may not be a particularly noble way to spend one's money. But on the other hand it no longer seems impossible. I'm not sure I would have a face-lift, but I can see having my eyes done or doing the collagen injections."

"Plastic surgery is absolutely necessary for me and something I'm saving money for," said a single woman of forty-five. "If I were married, I might feel differently, but the packaging counts when you're single."

"The only thing stopping me is fear," admitted one woman. "Surgery is a risk, and I can't see taking the risk to look younger."

"It's interesting," commented one fifty-year-old woman whose children had left home for good. "In so many ways I'm less consumer oriented, less material than I was ten years ago. I spend less money on clothes and makeup. I want a simpler life. But on the other hand I plan to have a face-lift in three or four years. I want always to look as good as I can."

A woman who had treated herself to eye surgery as a fiftieth-birthday present related her experience. "It was done in the doctor's office, and I was very nervous, thinking about something going wrong and affecting my eyes. But the doctor was extremely casual. Obviously this was all in a day's work for him. He gave me injections to deaden the area and also something to relax me. The whole procedure took about an hour, and I was bruised for about a week, and that was it. I was thrilled with the results. It was a very tiny little change that took years off my age and gave me that extra boost of confidence when I most needed it."

But another woman told of experiencing panic and pain when she tried collagen injections. "It hurt so much I was climbing off the table. I couldn't believe I had talked myself into a situation where I was letting someone put needles in my face. I stopped partway through my first treatment and have decided to accept my lines gracefully."

"I have thought about plastic surgery," admitted a fifty-three year-old woman, "but I'm not sure. I'm turned off to the idea because I'm afraid it will make me look grotesque . . . 'done.' It angers me that I have to think about it at all."

I liked the thoughtful way one woman looked at plastic surgery. "We tend to be moralistic about spending time on our physical appearance, because we judge this to be a superficial matter. But I think we've reached a point in our feminist development where we've come to understand that there's no moral question about deciding to wear makeup or dye your hair or have plastic surgery. Doing things to enhance your appearance does not make you a vapid person. Every woman has to evaluate these decisions for herself. What I would be careful of, if I were considering plastic surgery, would be that I didn't harbor unrealistic expectations that a change in my looks would radically alter my life for the better. It's possible to be too obsessed about buying back youth. It can't be done, and we shouldn't try."

Perhaps what we fear most, as we experience the aging of our bodies, is that we will be denied the pleasures of our sexuality. They seem to be inextricably linked—youth, beauty, and who we are as sexual beings. And as feminist writer Inge Powell Bell writes in an article entitled "The Double Standard: Age," this struggle is unique to women. For men, says Bell, "sexual value is defined much more in terms of personality, intelligence, and earning power than physical appearance. Women, however, must rest their case largely on their bodies. . . . The young girl of eighteen or twenty-five may well believe that her position in society is equal to, or even higher than, that of men. As she approaches middle age, however, she begins to notice a change in the way people treat her. Reflected in the growing indifference of others toward her looks, toward her sexuality, she can see and measure the decline of her worth. . . ."

This false standard is no doubt reinforced by our society's general lack of enlightenment about sexuality and our embarrassment about matters pertaining to sex—particularly our sense that it is somehow undignified to seek sexual pleasure after a certain age.

In reality sexuality is an essential part of our identities, from birth to death. While the way we express our sexuality changes as we pass through different stages of our lives, we do not become less sexual as we grow older. To say that would be akin to saying that we become less human or less female. In *The Eternal Garden—Seasons of Our Sexuality*, Sally Wendkos Olds identifies a series of sexual turning points that occur during our lives, each one equally valid and unique. Olds describes the fifties as a period when a number of other concerns—female menopause and its male equivalent, the emptying of the nest, changes in physical appearance and function—form the context of women's sexual experience. Olds also notes that the middle years can be a time of both sexual vulnerability and sexual exploration. Some women launch affairs during this period to gain assurance that they are still desirable. Others may decide it's their last chance for a fulfillment they never achieved in marriage. Still others may experience a new freedom once they no longer have concerns about birth control. Writes Olds: "The affairs that begin in mid-life may spring from any number of reasons. People who have been married for twenty years or so are likely to be feeling a sense of sameness to their lives, a sense that they keep doing the same things over and over again, that one day is much like the one that went before, that one week is like the last, that this year will duplicate last year."

It occurs to me that in most popular media mid-life sexual exploration is regarded as primarily a male domain. And even though men in their middle years who have affairs may be responding to dissatisfaction with the sameness Olds describes, as well as to a confrontation with their mortality, we, as women, find it hard to accept that their wandering eyes are not a judgment against us. Women frequently blame themselves when their men have affairs. Specifically as they grow older, they blame their declining desirability and secretly wonder how any man can be attracted to them when there are so many younger, fresher women available.

❉ ❉

Elizabeth is fifty-four, a wonderfully healthy-looking woman whose tall, warmly curved body seems to brim with energy and life. She and her husband, Tom, who is five years older, have lived in a small New Mexico city for twenty-five years and have worked compatibly for the past fifteen years in their small bookstore-newsstand.

Elizabeth likes to talk about the time, six years ago, when she and Tom weathered a great crisis. She believes the experience enabled them to come to terms with the important values in their relationship. And she credits the experience with teaching her a lesson about love and beauty that she had been unable to learn in all the years that predated the crisis. Today a serenity that was not there before pervades their lives.

"I was truly up against it then," Elizabeth says. "I was nearly fifty years old, and I felt I looked it. And, as a further insult, I had lost a breast the year before as a result of breast cancer. It was a period of great crisis for me. Tom was very tender and compassionate, but I was blind to everything but my own fears. You know how sometimes a person can tell you over and over that you're beautiful, but you just don't believe it? I turned away from Tom and turned inward upon myself.

"Losing the breast was not the beginning of my crisis. For at least two years prior to that I had begun to worry about my looks. Tom had always loved the way I looked, but I secretly believed that now he was only forcing himself. As my hips spread and my stomach sagged in the aftermath of carrying five children, I could feel only shame and embarrassment. I began to take great pains to avoid having Tom see me naked, especially from the back. In bed I would never lie on my side, because my stomach sagged so bad that it made me look pregnant. Instead I'd lie on my back and hold my breath to achieve the illusion of tightness.

"Then the breast. I wasn't afraid of dying. I was strong and healthy, and I knew I could overcome the cancer. But I was horrified by the insult to my body. Tom had always loved my breasts, and they were the only thing I wasn't ashamed of these days. Now I was lopsided and left only with a deep, purple scar where my beautiful breast used to be.

"I wouldn't let Tom see it for the longest time, and when I

finally showed it to him I watched his face carefully, knowing that he would shudder. How could one not shudder? But I was looking for the confirmation in his eyes of the death of my sexual appeal. I wouldn't let Tom have his grief. I treated his horror as an affront to me rather than as a natural response to the horror of cancer. And after that I wouldn't let him touch me, because I thought surely he was only forcing himself, and I was not about to be the object of anyone's pity.

"After I was fitted with a prosthesis, I returned to work at the store, taking great care with my appearance. There was a defiance in my behavior that manifested itself in casual flirting with the customers. I craved the attention of the men who came into the store. I needed their appreciative looks to confirm that I was still a woman.

"There was one man, in particular, a professor at the nearby college, who seemed very interested in me. He was a tall, good-looking man in his fifties, and we would often chat about politics and what was happening in the world. I liked the way he seemed to appreciate the whole me—not just my body but my mind as well. One day he asked me if I would have coffee with him, and I took a break and did it. Over coffee I told him about my surgery, and he marveled that he would never had known— I looked so healthy and natural. In fact, he told me, he had always been very attracted to me. He asked me how my husband had reacted when I had my surgery, and in great betrayal to Tom I shrugged and said, 'Oh, you know men. A woman who is missing a breast isn't much of a woman.' He took my hand and looked into my eyes and said, 'That's nonsense. Let me show you.'

"I pulled my hand away, but I was gratified. Wasn't this what I had been looking for—the assurance that men still found me desirable? We began to meet for coffee about once a week. He was married, and he often bent my ear about his wife and how much she had changed. I wondered if he realized when he talked about his wife he might as well have been describing me. I was the same age as she, and I had changed too. I began to hear myself defending her. 'Can't you see that she might be feeling insecure?' I asked, and he would only reply, 'But what about me?'

"You might say that eventually I came to my senses about this man. I began to take his complaints about his wife personally, because a man so indifferent to his wife's pain would be incapable of being anything more for another woman. And I also realized that Tom, who was far from indifferent, had never turned his back on me, even when I denied him the intimacy of my thoughts and physical presence.

"And so I experienced a watershed. And after that I gathered my courage, and for the first time I had a totally frank discussion with Tom about my feelings. To his credit, he did not wave aside my fears and call them silly. But he reminded me that, as he grew older, he had fears of his own to conquer and suggested that we do this fear-conquering together rather than working at cross-purposes. One thing Tom said was especially meaningful to me. He told me, 'I won't say it's "just" a breast, because I know that breast represents a tremendous loss. But you're more than your breast, so its loss doesn't make you all that different in my eyes.' And then he laughed and rubbed the bald area on top of his head. 'Am I just my hair?' he asked me."

Elizabeth's journey of self-awareness was perhaps more sharply defined by her cancer. But her story can serve as an example to all women who struggle with their looks and their sexuality during the transition from youth to aging.

※ ※

What does beauty mean for the middle-aged woman? There are so many mixed messages and questions that have no clear answers.

Should we shake off the signs of our aging, buy back our youth with plastic surgery or collagen injections or expensive creams?

Or should we "grow old gracefully," content in the belief that our lines and sags are in themselves beautiful?

Will there ever be a time when a mature woman in this society can truly feel good about herself and take pride in being the age she is?

Perhaps fifty is a good age to begin actively keeping our vanity in check so we can concentrate on other aspects of our lives that we hold valuable. It helps to choose a role model for growing older—Helen Hayes is one that women often mention, as is the writer May Sarton. My own role model, Georgia O'Keeffe, reminds me that there is more, much more, to my value as a woman than the way I look. Somehow lines begin to take on a different meaning when I think of how they looked on O'Keeffe's face. They were striking, artful.

Women who have been beautiful (in the manner that beauty is defined in our culture) often have a harder time with the aging process than women who have not been so notable in their looks. A woman who has depended on her youthful beauty to make her feel special will have to find a new self-story. This is not always so easy. Greta Garbo went into seclusion when she turned fifty-five. I once had a patient who could not bring herself to accept the decline of her beauty. She was obsessed by it, and her obsession reached the point where she could not look at old photo albums, because seeing the reflection of her former beauty drove her to tears.

Sometimes a desperate need to hold on to physical beauty indicates that a person has many regrets about the past. The subconscious rationalization is "If I can stay young-looking, I can turn back the clock and have a second chance." Women who are able to let go of their regrets about the past and look forward to what they can accomplish in the future will have less trouble with the changes that aging brings to their appearance.

To some extent all women are affected by the popular ideals, but we do not have to be victimized by negative cultural stereotypes. I believe that the first step we must take is to stop glorifying female youth in our own hearts. We don't need to accept the image portrayed by the woman in the beauty cream advertisement, who snarls into the camera, saying "I don't intend to grow old gracefully. I intend to fight it every step of the way."

I think K. C. Cole was referring to this sense of panic when she wrote in a *Ms.* magazine article, "Aging Bull," ". . . I worry about the contortions we feel we have to go through in the name of youth—the painful Retin A treatments, the disfiguring face and body lifts, which . . . carry a low but definitely not trivial risk of death or brain damage from anesthesia. Mummies look pretty good for their age, too. But there must be a limit to how far we'll go to keep ourselves carefully preserved."

Cole doesn't suggest that women should not try to look their best. We all have our particular little vanities, and plastic surgery isn't necessarily a bad thing. Rather it's the panic that Cole is addressing, the overwhelming fear that our sexual appeal is slipping away. Perhaps no man will love us once we show the signs of age. Perhaps men will be repulsed by the idea of our mature bodies.

Frances Lear, the publisher of *Lear's* magazine, suggests that mature women take a hard look at the message that the beauty-youth industries are sending. "Our antiwrinkle creams are advertised on seventeen-year-old faces," she says. "Our clothes—ours because they are appropriate or because they are expensive, or both—are modeled on size-six bodies, on women often younger than our daughters. Women in their twenties pose alongside our cars. Our household products are demonstrated in commercials by very young actors or actors who are caricatures. Why are we getting shoved around like this?"

Good question. It is clear that we are, at least in part, to blame for the stereotypes because we allow them and believe in them ourselves. But Lear reminds us that we have the power to change the stereotypes and introduce a new paradigm for beauty. "History," says Lear, "as written in great part by women themselves, has forced us to enter brave new worlds bravely. And when we have, we have prevailed. Triumph and mastery are giving contemporary women an inner beauty that defines real beauty nowadays and sets aside, perhaps for all time, superficial beauty as the symbol of the Youth Culture, the icon of the unseasoned self."

Linked with our worries over fading physical beauty is the fear that an aging body is a nonsexual body. The myth that sexuality declines as our bodies age remains a predominant one in our society. But what are the facts?

According to the newsletter *Sex Over Forty*, published by PHE, Inc., being older can actually prove to be an advantage when it comes to sex. According to the newsletter several studies confirm the fact that, as women grow older, they become more comfortable with sex, they enjoy sex more, they are more likely to be orgasmic, and they are more likely to be vaginally orgasmic. Although the women I interviewed did not always say the felt more enjoyment from sex as they grew older, I can appreciate the validity of the studies. An older woman may well find that she is able to relax and enjoy sex more fully. She can do this with a partner she trusts—true in many long-term relationships—and she may no longer have to have concerns about using contraception. To be sure, there are physical changes that can affect sexual pleasure. There is less vaginal lubrication, and the vaginal walls may become thinner. But those changes are easy enough to overcome. More damaging to sexual pleasure is self-image. And our youth-oriented society has brainwashed many women to believe that it is shameful to want and enjoy sex after a certain age or that their bodies become less desirable to men.

What we so often forget—and our youth- and body-obsessed society makes it easy to forget—is that sexuality and sexual appeal are matters of great complexity that transcend physical appearance and age. The sources of human sexual attraction cannot be attributed simplistically to physical appearance. They are multifaceted and, ultimately, very personal.

We also often fail to see the ways in which our changing sexuality is a good thing. When we are ashamed about growing older, it is reflected in everything we do, and shame can sap our vitality. But if we learn to tap into the fullness of our age, whatever age that may be, we communicate an entirely different impression—that of a woman who is confident and secure in her maturity, who enjoys having reached a point of familiarity and comfort with her body and with sex.

"The year I turned fifty was also the year I had my first sexual experience with a man other than my husband," Lee, a fifty-three-year-old widow, told me. "Jim, my husband, was the first and only man I had ever had sex with. We had a good sex life, and I never wanted another man. It also never occurred to me that I wouldn't be with Jim forever. He died of a heart attack at fifty-two, and suddenly I was alone but not feeling old enough to give up having sex. I had gone through menopause early and wasn't having my period anymore. An old friend of ours, who was divorced, invited me out to dinner. Steve was someone I had always found to be attractive, and I felt great when he told me he found me attractive too. Jim had been dead for a year at this point, and we both missed him, but the grief was fading. We started spending time together, and gradually the conversation was less about Jim and more about us. At some point I realized that we were probably going to be having sex, and I was very scared. I wasn't sure I knew how to do it right. All I knew was what Jim and I had done. But my biggest fear was that Steve wouldn't like my body. I had kept in pretty good shape, but there were things that just couldn't be stopped. My breasts sagged some, and so did my butt. I had wrinkles and varicose veins, and my upper arms wiggled. When I looked at myself in the mirror, all of these flaws became magnified a thousand times.

"The big moment finally came one night when I was having dinner at Steve's house. I started to undress, and I was kind of backing away from him so he wouldn't see my butt, and holding a hand under my breasts to lift them a little, and flexing my arms so they would look less flabby—and the whole time my mind was busy with what he could possibly be thinking. And he smiled and came over to where I was standing in this awkward position, and he said, 'You're beautiful.' I could see he meant it, and at that moment years of worry flew out of me and I relaxed. Later I realized that Steve did not see my body as a separate thing from *me*. He loved me as a complete package. I guess I always thought men walked around with little mental checklists that said 'breasts too small . . . hips too flabby,' but Steve never even noticed those things. If I called his attention to them, which I did later out of insecurity, he laughed and said I was being silly. We're still together, and we're going to get married, and after three years I'm finally convinced that Steve finds me sexually attractive because I'm me, wrinkles and all."

When Lee told me this story, I rejoiced to hear such a clear expression of victory over fear and self-denigration. What a wonderful thing it would be if all of us could just let go of the nagging doubts, let go of the need to examine ourselves in well-lit mirrors, wrinkle by wrinkle and sag by sag, let go of the fear that the men we love and the people with whom we work are judging us critically. Lee's experience reinforced the reasons I wanted so much to write this book. She talks about this period of her life as the beginning of a new chapter, one that is filled with the excitement of the unknown. In that respect the adolescent girl, fresh in her new womanhood, and the menopausal woman share the same experience of standing on the brink of a mysterious new period in their lives when anything is possible.

BEING BEAUTIFUL AT FIFTY

The mid-life woman of the nineties is neither body-obsessed nor body-ignorant. She shares the common health consciousness of the times—is knowledgeable about diet, exercise, and the other considerations that keep her healthy—knowing too that health is a necessary component of style and sexuality. Cosmetic and health considerations go hand in hand when you think about what it means to be beautiful in mid-life. And a good place to start is to evaluate the shape you're in and make some changes in the way you live. These changes can have a direct effect on the way you look now and the rate at which you will physically age. For example:

If you smoke, now is the time to stop. Smoking not only affects your health; it also causes your face to age faster.

If you drink, keep it moderate.

If you haven't already developed one, investigate what a balanced, healthful diet looks like for you. Many women have lived their adult lives going on and off extreme weight-loss diets. Now is the time to eat for health and be sure that you're getting enough of the nutrients you need—such as calcium.

Regular aerobic exercise will not only keep you looking good; it will improve your cardiovascular fitness as well. This is crucial, because heart disease is the number-one ailment to afflict midlife Americans—both males *and* females. There is also solid evidence that aerobic exercise prevents osteoporosis.

Once you have made the necessary changes in your life to improve your health and fitness, it is a good idea to take inventory of your style—the "face" you're going to present to the world. This goes much deeper than the cosmetic. Your energy, creativity, warmth, and personality are the vital underpinnings of who you are, and in that respect an "inner makeover" is just as important as an outer makeover. But I think that fifty is a good age to reevaluate some aspects of your appearance, and perhaps make changes. Maybe the way you've worn your hair and makeup for the last twenty years is no longer the most flattering look for you, and it's time to experiment with something different.

And what about plastic surgery? That's a personal matter—some women feel comfortable with it and others don't. But if you're interested in exploring it as a possibility, there are many options. Plastic surgery has become very common and more accessible to the average woman, as have nonsurgical treatments such as collagen implants. Some people consider plastic surgery a denial of the natural aging process, but I disagree. There is nothing inherently good or bad about plastic surgery. If you want to do it and can afford to do it, there is nothing wrong with trying to improve your appearance. But keep in mind that plastic surgery is serious business—it is surgery. And you should use the same care in choosing a plastic surgeon as you would in choosing any other medical specialist. If you don't know where to start, ask your personal physician for a recommendation. Or call your local hospital or medical society. Be sure the doctor you choose is certified by the American Board of Plastic Surgery. That will guarantee that he or she is an M.D. who has had special additional training.

Before you visit a plastic surgeon, do some research of your own so you'll have a complete list of questions to take with you to the visit. You'll want to know exactly what you can expect—not just the final results but also the procedure and recovery period. Ask the doctor for names and phone numbers of women he or she has operated on. Call and talk to them about their experience. Don't be shy. You will learn a lot.

Above all, as you are considering plastic surgery or any other beautifying treatments, always stay in touch with who you are. Find ways of affirming your uniqueness, the things that really make you beautiful and sexy, inside and out. Think of this time of your life not in terms of what you have lost but in terms of what you have gained. Don't deny yourself the chance to let go of some of the old fears about your body that may have been holding you back in the past. For example, if you have spent many years being obsessed about your weight and trying to be thin, this might be a good time to give up that obsession and discover what it feels like to live in the body you have, not the one you wish you had.

If you are afraid to try this, it might comfort you to know that in my years of practice I've discovered that many men are less obsessed with thinness and youth in women than what the stereotypes suggest. When the outer layers of their defenses are stripped away, men and women alike find that what they really seek is a feeling of wholeness that comes from having a strong sense of identity and being able to share oneself intimately with another person. Often we lose sight of that in our quest for youth and beauty, and often older men, who may themselves be feeling insecure about their sexuality and appeal, need women to help show them it's okay to be older.

And sometimes, in an ironic twist, these issues take care of themselves. One fifty-year-old woman in Santa Barbara saved her money for years "so when I reached this age, I could afford to go into therapy and learn to accept getting older—or, failing that, pay for plastic surgery." She laughed as she revealed what finally happened. "I married a man who is fifteen years older than me, and now I feel young enough just the way I am."

❦ 5 ❦
Beyond the Mother Role

New Orleans at the height of Mardi Gras is a dizzying spectacle, alive with color, jubilance, and the throbbing pulse of a frenzied mob. It was something I had always wanted to see, and now here I was sitting in Sharon's yard, with three of her friends, five miles north of the French Quarter.

I had wanted to meet with a group of Southern women because I felt that their experiences might be different from those of other women in the country. Typically, it seems, Southern women have an unmistakable mystique—the soft, pliable sweetness edged with a hard-as-nails strength that is very attractive. Sharon was a classic example. An accomplished university professor and published author, she appeared at first glance to be fragile as fine china.

Her friends, Mary, Olivia, and Angela, also appeared to be classic Southern women—managing at the same time to possess a sense of cool control and an appealing gentility. Mary, a statuesque blond of forty-eight, was trying to get her life back together after a recent divorce. Olivia, a fifty-year-old black woman, had been divorced for many years and worked in a stylish boutique. Angela, also fifty, was a successful travel agent, married to a lawyer.

We were all mothers of adult or nearly adult children, and the conversation began casually around the subject of our offspring. Angela was talking about her son, who had decided to take a year off from college to work. "I wish he wouldn't," she said, frowning with worry. "My husband doesn't think there's anything wrong with the idea, but I'm afraid he'll lose his momentum at school. Everything is so competitive these days. I keep telling myself that John—that's my son—is twenty years old and can make his own decisions. But I don't really believe it."

"I know what you mean," I said. "It's hard to let go. I have had to force myself to stand back and allow my children their independence, knowing that they will make mistakes. My daughter is away at college in another part of the state, and until recently, whenever I spoke with her on the phone I found myself quizzing her about what she'd eaten, whether she'd eaten. I still wanted to keep that link of taking care of her, but she was beyond my care. It was hard for me to accept that she didn't need me or want me in the same way anymore."

"I know I'm an overprotective mother," Angela admitted. "I just don't want my children to make the same mistakes I made. I also think life is more dangerous out there than it was thirty years ago. A lot of kids who are kicked out of the nest can't make it on their own. I worry about this, so I tend to resist encouraging them to be independent. I keep the house open for them." She grimaced. "Right now our whole house is packed with sleeping college kids because of Mardi Gras."

"For me it's kind of a back-and-forth thing," said Olivia. "My children have always understood that they were to be independent. When they reminisce, they remember having made doctors' appointments for themselves when they were only eight years old. They weren't that young, of course. But I've always encouraged them to do things on their own. Now I have one daughter who recently moved to Boston, and I haven't heard from her for two months. My other daughter called me last night to ask if she could eat something that's been in the refrigerator for two weeks without getting food poisoning. It's one extreme or the other."

"Being a mother is a hard habit to break," said Angela with a laugh. "When everyone is home, I fall back into the old mother role and my children fall back into the old 'What's for dinner?' thing. I just did two loads of laundry this morning. I can't get over the notion that I'm being a bad mother if I don't do these things for them. If the kids need me for anything, that's the number-one priority. Part of it is because I love it and I love them. I miss them when they're away."

Sharon, fifty-three, grimaced. "I agree, but am I the only one here who sometimes feels like I've been demoted from mother to secretary? I take their phone messages, readdress their mail as they move around, keep their things stored."

We all laughed. It was a common theme. "But," Sharon went on, holding up a hand, "I've tried hard to live with it. Whenever I start feeling sorry for myself, I remember back—it hasn't been *that* long—to how I felt when I was their age. I left home without a backward glance. I loved my parents, but they weren't the center of my life. They represented what was familiar, and I was dying to try everything in sight that was new."

"Besides, they'd always be there," added Angela. "For later, when you needed them. Just like we'll always be there for our children."

"What do you think is the best kind of relationship for us to have with our adult children?" I asked. "I think we're reinventing this role too."

"Supportive," said Sharon, "but more than friendship. My children still call on me sometimes to be their mother, and I enjoy helping them now that I no longer think of it as such an obligation."

"My daughter has opened me up to new ideas," said Olivia. "As our children reach adulthood, we have to be willing to treat them as people with valid ways of thinking and behaving. For example, my daughter got involved in feeding the homeless, and she got me involved last year, cooking and taking food to the center. It was meaningful—and something I would not have thought of doing on my own. I'm wondering now if I might have a different relationship with my children—something closer to mutual appreciation and friendship."

"My children have been informed that at age twenty-two, six months after college graduation, they will be on their own," said Mary firmly, and everyone laughed. "It's not that I won't be supportive, and they can stay in the house if they need to. But the difference is it will be on my terms or not at all."

I brought up the subject of money, knowing it was a touchy area where adult children are concerned.

"I'm like a bank," said Mary. "I will loan money to my kids if I think they're a good credit risk. I'm not going to put myself in the position of feeling angry when they don't pay me back. My former husband is very generous with the kids, and they go to him. He never turns them down for anything—especially since we've been divorced. I don't agree with that position, because I think that at a certain point they need to know that they have to live on what they're earning. When you just give them money whenever they ask, it negates their own pride in discovering what they can do for themselves."

"Money becomes a difficult issue because we want so much to give our children everything we can," I suggested. "We don't want to deprive them. Yet, at the same time, we care that they learn for themselves how to be responsible. I know a woman who faced a crisis when her son, a sophomore in college, was doing poorly in his studies. She and her husband had always assumed they would pay for his college, and even for graduate school, if he wanted it. But they came to the conclusion that he wasn't holding up his end of the deal. So they changed the arrangement. They told their son he would have to pay for his tuition and then, for every course in which he got a C or better, they would refund the money. This was a radical move, and they were scared to make it, but it turned out pretty well. Their son had to quit school for a semester to raise the initial money, but he's doing better now. And the woman told me that one of the benefits has been that her son really appreciates how expensive an education is these days. So it's been a learning and growing experience."

"I like that plan," said Olivia. "I think we have to let our children know that we're there for them, but they have responsibilities too. We're not doing them a favor if we don't teach them to stand on their own."

"I've found that one way to get at how independent your children really are is to consider their relationship to you and your home," I said. "In other words, do you still think of them as living there even though they now have their own homes? Do you still allow them to intrude on your life whenever they want? Do they still have keys to your home?"

"I let the same ones have keys that I would loan money to," Mary said with a grin. "Really, it isn't just automatic—it's a matter of trust."

"Do the kids who don't have keys accept the fact that some do?" asked Angela. "I would hate to risk alienating my children over something like that."

"They know the reasons," said Mary. "I have two kids I won't let have keys to the house, because in the past they have brought friends over who have stolen from me. When my kids moved out into apartments of their own—which, incidentally, I don't have keys to—I asked for their keys back in a routine way. It's not a big issue. I hid a key outside and let only those I trusted know where I hid it. If they didn't like it, tough. When my daughter started living with a boy I didn't know anything about, I moved the key. I don't think there's anything wrong with needing to feel safe in my own house—especially since I live alone. I explained it to my children as being a privacy issue. They wouldn't want me to have keys to their apartments, would they? Or to be able to just show up without calling? Somehow in that context, they understood it better. I really believe these boundaries help adult children cut the ties and get on with their own lives. If it's too easy to go home again, no one wins."

"It's hard to set limits," I said. "I think Angela voiced a fear that is very real for most of us. We don't want our children to be angry and alienated. Sometimes we're afraid to take the chance and assert ourselves. There's always the nagging thought 'What if they get mad and go away forever?' I remember an incident when my son was in college. There was a long-standing rule that there would be no dogs in the house, and he had a dog at school. Two weeks before Christmas he informed me that the only way he would come home would be if he could bring Razz with him. I knew he was testing me. I'm sure he thought I would cave in if it came to the point where my rule would prevent him from coming. But I stuck to my guns, and he ended up putting Razz in a kennel, paying for it, and coming home."

Everyone applauded me for sticking to my guns, and I thought, wryly, how in hindsight what I had done was so simple and right, while at the time it had seemed to be such a loaded cannon. "Nothing's simple when it happens," I shrugged. "We're always feeling our way. Now, something else I want to ask is whether any of you have adult children who have returned home. This has become a big subject these days. A recent statistic I read from the Census Bureau estimated that, among twenty-five- to twenty-nine-year olds, 16 percent of the men and 8 percent of the women were living with their parents or having their living expenses paid for. Anyone here?"

All four women shook their heads no. "It might happen to me," said Angela. "My husband and I have offered to let our son live with us after he finished school until he gets settled."

"As I mentioned before, I don't believe in it," said Mary. "I think it's just a way of doing everything for them instead of letting them find the answers for themselves."

"Oh, I don't think it's that," protested Angela. "Why shouldn't we help out if we can?"

"We should," said Mary. "But at some point the birds have to leave the nest. Sometimes I wonder if we do too much for our children. My parents could never afford to do much for me, so I didn't expect it, and I did okay. I'm glad I had the chance to learn to make it on my own. I feel strongly that my children should have a similar experience."

"Let's face it," I said. "Many adult children are returning home to live after college these days because they can't afford to live on their own. What is our responsibility to our adult children?"

"I think it has to be planned for," suggested Sharon. "I have a friend who made a contract with her son and kept it very businesslike. She rented him a room for $150 a month, including meals, and he had to do his own cooking, cleaning, and laundry. The contract spelled out his rights as a 'tenant' as well as her rights to have her home the way she wanted it. Their contract is renewable every year, because she also doesn't want him living there forever."

"That's a good idea," said Mary, "but even a contract doesn't assure that you will stop mothering—if you know what I mean."

I nodded. "Even when our children are adults, we have to guard against the urge to meddle inappropriately and make their decisions for them. One woman, whose twenty-five-year-old son lives at home, told me how difficult it was for her. She described how one morning her son, who has a job in an advertising agency, overslept. She wanted to knock on his door and get him up so he wouldn't be late for work, but she resisted the impulse because she realized that was his responsibility now.

"I recently learned that the organization Outward Bound was patterned after a British tradition. Wealthy families sent their teenage sons out to sea for a year so that they could learn survival skills and not become softened by their lifestyles of privilege. Throughout history it's been an issue for parents: how much to give a child and how much is too much."

"I like that example," Mary said. "Eventually our children are going to have to learn to overcome obstacles without our help. Why not prepare them for it?"

"There's no right or wrong answer," I said. "Each family has its own circumstances. But I will say that you have to think carefully about how to relate to adult children living in your home. From what you've said already, Angela, it seems that you might have to fight against the tendency to do everything for them—laundry, cooking . . ."

"True." Angela smiled.

"On the other hand, sometimes having your children home as adults gives you a chance to get to know them on another level. The trick is to respect them as adults and to insist that they respect your life too. It's easy for both parents and children to revert to the ways they behaved when the children were younger."

"A friend of mine did that with her daughter," Olivia said. "My, how she used to bend my ear! Her daughter would stay out half the night, and she was a bundle of nerves. Mind you, that girl was twenty-six years old, but the woman worried herself half to death. She also complained a lot because the girl wouldn't wash a dish if her life depended on it. Once I told her, 'Why don't you lay down the law and tell your daughter the way it's going to be if she chooses to live with you?' but she wouldn't do it. She didn't want her daughter to leave."

"Another thing I've noticed about the time when our children begin to move away is the question of how that changes the space we live in," I said. "Do you leave things the same, or do you use their rooms? Do you ask them to take their belongings, or do you store them? I suppose it seems like a minor issue, but I suspect it represents several larger issues, including our willingness to let go of our children and their willingness to be completely independent from us. It also relates to the new sense of freedom we feel as our children leave home. Many women have described to me their eagerness to get rid of all the stuff that has tied them down."

"We dealt with that by moving," said Sharon. "This house has room for everyone, but it's a different house. They don't have their own niches here. It's not their home anymore."

"Did it bother them when you moved?" I asked.

"Oh, yes—it was funny, really. My daughter said, 'Mother, how you can do this—leave our home?' I had to remind her that it was no longer *her* home. Our needs were more important, and we wanted to be closer to the city. It helped that I warned her far in advance about the move, and told her it would mean she wouldn't have her own room anymore, although there would be guest rooms."

"It's good that you gave her notice," I said. "It's a terrible mistake to dismantle a child's room and think he or she won't care. It must be done eventually, and it's good if the child has time to get used to the idea."

"Children think your life is going to stand still while they change," said Mary. "It makes them a little nervous when you start breaking the mold. Being divorced, I see it more than others. I've reached the point where I don't tell them much about my social life. They don't like to imagine their mother going out on dates."

"I have to admit that it's been a real struggle for me to relate to my children as they get older," said Sharon, rubbing her eyes wearily. "Right now my oldest is trying to separate by not talking to me. She's got a long list of grievances that she repeats often. Finally I said to her, 'I've heard this too many times, and these things all happened in the past. Some are true and accurate, and I did them because I didn't know any better. But it's time to stop this and leave them behind you and get on with your life.'"

"You probably saved her ten years of therapy," Mary said, laughing.

"She agreed with me, and things got better for a while. She even came home from school to help celebrate my fiftieth birthday. But then she left without saying good-bye, so I guess it's not over yet."

"That's the hardest," said Olivia sympathetically. "When they keep such a distance. It's almost better to have the fights than it is to have them not be there or not call. I went through a period like that with my daughter. Nothing I could say or do seemed right. We were drifting apart, and there was nothing I could do to stop it. But after a while things seemed to work out on their own."

"It's not easy to achieve objectivity when it comes to our children," I mused. "Whether we are aware of it on a conscious level or not, they are so much a part of validating who we are. I had an experience a few months ago that really brought that home for me. My daughter, Kim, was home from school on a visit, and we were in the kitchen. I was over at the stove heating water for tea, and Kim was sitting at the table eating a sandwich. Suddenly I heard choking sounds, and I spun around and Kim was gagging and waving her arms. Her face had turned blue. I froze for an instant, then I reached for the phone. My first thought was to call for help; then I realized there was no time for that. I was watching my daughter die. I ran over to her and did the Heimlich maneuver, and a piece of tomato popped from her throat. She started crying, and I was crying. We held each other. Neither of us stopped shaking for hours. And I thought, 'My God, it's all so fragile. In an instant everything could have been wiped out.'"

"That suddenly they could be gone," Sharon said, nodding. "It's so unthinkable. I don't know how parents ever adjust to losing a child. It would make life seem so senseless."

"Yes, that's what occurred to me at the time," I said. "It's so contrary to the nature of things—or what we think of as the nature of things: that the parents precede their children to the grave."

"I wonder if I would want to live in a world that didn't include my children," Angela said quietly.

Mary nodded. "I think most of us agree, and yet I find myself increasingly establishing my distance from them, as though their turn for attention is over and now it is my turn. And sometimes this makes me feel guilty, because although I do not love them less, it might seem that way to them."

※ ※

We have been called the "sandwich generation." Our children and our parents sometimes seem to hem us in from both sides. They demand our attention, our care, our love, and these things, once so easy to give, seem suddenly available in more meager supply. A friend of mine once said, in what I judged to be a cynical view, that there are two kinds of love: the love we have for those whose lives we can control and the love we have for those who control us. Children and parents.

I do not believe it is true that I love my children less now that they are no longer in my control. Just differently. When they were young, they were joined to me so closely. Their spare minutes belonged to me and mine to them. When we were not together, I thought of them hundreds of times every hour; my daily lists were filled with the evidence of their need for me—the purchase of new shoes, props for a school play, trips to the dentist. When we were together, they crowded into my space. Every decision, large or small, included them. I knew where they were every minute. Then, later, I watched them gradually move away, and I felt a jolt of loss as I realized that I could never have those earlier times back. If, in some ways, my children remained the center of my life, I saw that I no longer remained the center of theirs. The shape of our conversations changed; they were more guarded. They were great kids, but, like all teenagers, they fought for their independence. I may have still retained some control over their actions, but I could not break in on the privacy of their thoughts. Our conversations often yielded no information:

"How was your day?
"Fine."
"What's wrong?"
"Nothing."
"Where are you going?"
"Out."
"Who are you going with?"
"Oh—just friends."

When my brow would furrow with the fears my imagination inspired, they would laugh, pat me on the back, and think I was being silly. "Don't worry, Mom. I know what I'm doing."

I set rules for them and established curfews, but I never sat up waiting as some parents do. I did worry and felt, as all parents do, the push-pull of on the one hand maintaining authority and on the other hand allowing freedom.

Several years go, when I was writing *Intimate Secrets*—

Which to Keep and Which to Tell, I realized that an important aspect of the book needed to be devoted to the emergence of self that a child experiences. Much of that emergence is bound up in secrets, especially during the teenage years, which might also be called the "Who am I?" years. Of course there are many different types of secrecy; to a great extent a child responds to the signals that his or her parents give. But even the most wonderful, understanding parent in the world won't inspire the complete confidence of a young adult, who needs to establish his or her separateness. And letting go seems to be even more dangerous during the years when we are most called on to do so. There are so many scary unknowns out in the world. What parent does not desperately long to protect her children from harm or hurt?

I can understand, in a way, how some parents might create a defense against their fears of separation by building a wall between themselves and their children. They may try to convince themselves that they care less about them now that they are older. "Do what you want," they might say, "but don't come to me if you get into trouble."

I recently saw a movie about a young man who discovered that he had AIDS. Since he lived in a different city than his parents, he had been able to hide from them the fact that he was gay. In particular he believed that his father, a gruff, proud man, would never be able to accept it. The young man was his father's shining star; he couldn't bring himself to disappoint him. So he lived his secret life, visiting home during the holidays and pretending it didn't matter that his parents didn't know who he was, because they were proud of him and he gave them great pleasure.

But now he was dying, and he had nowhere to go but home. He had to tell them, because it was no longer his secret to keep.

His father's first reaction was to lunge at him in fury. Then, later, he shut the son out, refusing to speak to him. Finally the young man confronted his father, pleading for acceptance. "This is who I am," he said.

His father looked at him bitterly and said, "How dare you come here and ask me to accept who you are? I don't know who you are. You have kept your entire life—everything you've done and felt—a secret from me. You're a stranger."

In that moment the father's hurt crystallized. His grief was not so much for his son's revelation but for the realization that his son had chosen to be a stranger to the man who loved him more than anyone in the world.

Sometimes it feels like an impossible balance, encouraging our children to establish their separate identities while trying to remain close. As we sit on the sidelines of their lives, observing both their successes and their failures with a forced detachment, we hope that they will want to share with us the important things.

In the novel *Breathing Lessons* Anne Tyler gives us Maggie, a well-meaning, meddling mother, who is so single-minded in her perception of what is best for her son that she is blind to the growing body of evidence that what she wants for him is not what he wants. Maggie takes pleasure in being a manipulator; she sees it as her benevolent, motherly duty to maneuver her son and his estranged wife back together. She is stunned when she is told finally, bluntly, that it is not going to happen. It is not what anyone wants. Maggie had never considered that her prodding and manipulating were not appreciated. She protests that she was only trying to help, and she doesn't understand the nature of the accusations being leveled against her. The story leaves Maggie in a state of confusion and grief; she feels strangely invalidated by hearing the truth.

But it isn't just that our children are changing and growing independently of us. We too are changing, even if, like Maggie, we find the change occurring against our will. And we become different in relation to our children themselves now that we are no longer their caretakers. Suddenly, when our eyes meet across the table, it is with the shared understanding that exists between adults. There is a new pleasure in this sharing.

It is not just that we want to feel a closeness with our adult children. We also want them to appreciate us, to feel proud of us. During their teenage years our children are busy pulling away. Part of their emerging identity involves challenging our values, and this can make us feel that they think less of us. Teenagers are capable of communicating absolute disdain for their parents. Yet as they reach adulthood the balance shifts somewhat and it becomes possible for parents and their children to relate in entirely new ways. No longer as threatened by the authority figures that parents are in youth, children often are able to express new warmth. Being appreciated by your children is one of life's greatest moments, and it often happens around the fifty mark. I'll never forget how wonderful I felt while attending a ceremony for my daughter, Kim, at the State University at Cortland. The ceremony was for students who were at the top of the class, and my daughter was one of them—in the top 5 percent. I was so proud of her! But then there was an even more thrilling moment. The president of the university asked the students to stand and he had the parents applaud them. Then he asked the parents to stand and had the students applaud us. The clapping went on and on, and I looked into the face of my daughter, who was clapping furiously, and I felt we had turned a corner in our relationship. There wasn't a dry eye in the room!

I identified with Rachel, the mother in Jane Smiley's *Ordinary Love & Good Will,* who felt a sense of satisfaction when she casually mentioned a sexual matter to her twenty-five-year-old son. She did it deliberately, explaining that "this is something I've done all summer with Joe, refer to subjects usually taboo between mother and son. I would like my sons to make of me what I am, just an adult woman, but an adult woman in every way. I would like them to do me that favor, now, before they have wives." I glimpsed in Rachel's desire a new truth: that one of the things we want from our adult children is their appreciation of our womanly, feminine selves beyond the role that motherhood imposes. We want their love for us to take into account that we are flesh and blood and have the same longings as everyone else.

For most of us the time our children become adults also

signals the beginning of completely new roles for us, including those of becoming mothers-in-law and grandmothers.

Most women I interviewed spoke enthusiastically about becoming grandmothers, describing how much they could give to the children. Although most of them had careers and would not be the cookie-baking, baby-sitting grandmas of old, they were intrigued by the idea of what one woman called "New Age grandparenting." The fifty-year-old women who were already grandmothers said they loved their new role. Many had taken pains to set certain limits with their children before the babies were born regarding just how involved they planned to be. One woman mentioned that she enjoyed taking care of her grandchildren once a month "so the kids can get away alone." As she explained it, "My parents did that for us, and I feel good that we can give our children the same gift." But another woman insisted on just taking care of one grandchild at a time. Never very confident around children, she feels this is a way she can give each one special attention while not feeling overwhelmed herself. Another woman welcomes her grandchildren at any time, but they must be accompanied by a baby-sitter so she won't have to do everything for them.

Most of the women said that they enjoyed getting some of their "mothering/nurturing needs" met—with the advantage that they could return the children to their parents at the end of the visit.

A few women said that they felt guilty because they didn't want to be typical grandmothers—as one described it, "at home baking cookies." But they also said they felt they were reinventing the grandmother role, and that felt good. Open communication with their children seemed to be important here, and it wasn't always an easy issue to resolve.

One woman told me about a confrontation she had with her son. "He called and asked if I could take the baby for the weekend, and I said no because I was very tired. I'd had a hard week at work," she said. "He was upset. He said, 'What kind of a grandmother are you?' I realized that he was remembering the way my mother was always there when he and his brother were children. She lived a few blocks away and her door was always open. He was having a hard time adjusting his images to the reality of my life. I am a working grandmother, and my time is less available. After I refused to baby-sit, he grew very distant for a couple of weeks until I forced the issue by confronting him. Once we had discussed it, I was able to understand his feelings. He was afraid his child would never experience what he remembered as wonderful times with his grandmother. I assured him that I wanted to be an important part of my granddaughter's life, but in a different way than my mother had been for my children."

Yet, as enthusiastic as they were about becoming grandmothers, most women had given very little thought to becoming mothers-in-law, even though this new role usually comes first.

I admit that I have mixed feelings about becoming a mother-in-law. The stereotypes are so gruesome! When mother-in-law jokes cross my path, I instinctively flinch. "How do you tell good mushrooms from bad?" goes a joke I heard recently. "Feed them to your mother-in-law. If she dies, they're good." This joking is considered to be "all in good fun." I fail to find the humor or the fun.

If the ideal of motherhood is nurturing and benevolent, the image of the mother-in-law becomes the Medusa—critical, ill-intentioned, and mean in spirit. To some extent she is the scapegoat for the darker side of our feelings about our own mothers, which we do not feel free to express. The women interviewed were mostly able to accept their children's mates. They reported finding that their acceptance made it much easier.

As this book goes to press, two of Bob's daughters have gotten married and I have become a stepmother-in-law two times over. I'm not sure how this drama will play itself out; already I have felt the different status accorded to stepmothers as opposed to birth mothers. I went shopping for a dress, and when the saleswoman heard that I was not the mother of the bride, but the stepmother, she laughed and said, "Oh, well, then you just wear beige lace and keep your mouth shut." I didn't choose beige lace to wear at either wedding, but I have always kept my mouth shut and tried to be as supportive of the new couples as I could.

Weddings are chaotic times, and those of us in our middle years are bound to experience many mixed emotions. As we watch a whole new generation starting families, we might easily feel saddened by how fast our own lives have rushed by and how many of our youthful dreams have been left unfulfilled. But weddings also inspire us with their theme of new beginnings, and they allow us to expand our family limits and embrace new relatives. At weddings we see clearly that the chain of life goes on and that we have played an important part in keeping that chain growing.

BEING A GOOD MOTHER

Every woman wants to be a good mother, but we often fail to realize that what it means to be a good mother to a small child is very different from what it means to be a good mother to a young adult. You never stop being a mother, but your most important task, as your children reach adulthood, is to determine what it means to be a good mother now.

This struggle has been a recurring theme among nearly all of my women patients over the years, and I have learned that there were few guidelines available. It's hard for women to shift gears as their children grow, since no one has defined for them exactly how they are supposed to behave. A multitude of traps lie along the way, ready to ensnare you. The most common are guilt that you are not doing enough and fear that you are doing too much. If your identity has been linked closely with your role of caring for your children, you might wonder how you can demonstrate your closeness to them now that you are not doing as much. (It is this insecurity that drove one of my patients to continue doing laundry for her son well into his twenties.)

If you are struggling with this issue, don't forget yourself in the midst of your concerns for your children. You are not living their lives: you are living *your* life. Once your children reach adulthood, it is not only appropriate but also necessary that you put your own needs before theirs.

Perhaps you should also ask yourself what your heavy investment in your children implies. Are you using them as a shield against your own self-discovery? Are you living too much through them? Do you hesitate to let go for fear that you will have nothing of value remaining?

If you fear the "empty nest," the best thing to do is to take steps to fill it. One woman told how she and her husband, who was a college professor, enjoyed inviting students to their home so there would always be young people with fresh ideas around. She noted that each semester they "adopted" one or two students who became special to them. Another woman told of getting a dog when her youngest went away to college. "It helped me let go," she said, "while still having something to reduce the loneliness." These are creative solutions that help move people from one phase of their lives to another.

Most important, if you are willing to open up a new relationship with your children that is mother to adult rather than mother to child, you will find this new relationship to be wonderful and rewarding in an entirely different way.

❊ 6 ❊
Our Parents' Keepers

For many women the freedom of completing their child-rearing years is tempered by a new responsibility—that of being caretaker for aging parents. According to the Older Women's League (OWL), 72 percent of the caretakers of the elderly are women, an estimated 1.6 million. Says OWL president Lou Glasse, "The average woman today can expect to spend as many years caring for a dependent parent (or spouse) as she does in caring for a dependent child." Furthermore, according to Jannette K. Newhouse, extension specialist, Adult Development and Aging, Virginia Polytechnic Institute and State University-Blacksburg, the squeeze of generations makes their role more difficult. "Because family caregivers are most often mid-life and older women, it's not unusual for them to be caught between the competing demands of two adjacent generations," says Newhouse. "Not only do those giving care to frail elders endure role strain and confusion; they often experience increased financial stress, depression, and lack of substitute caregivers, making it difficult for them to leave home."

Another recent study, by Travelers Insurance Company, found that more of its employees were taking care of elderly relatives than were taking care of dependent children. According to Andrew Scharlach, Ph.D., who conducted the study, as the elderly population increases, this trend is expected to grow. Already, notes Scharlach, the fastest-growing segment of the United States population is the eighty-five-and-over age group. Other points of Scharlach's study are also worthy of note:

• Caregivers who are employed outside the home spend approximately as much time caring for elderly relatives as those who are not employed outside the home. They do it by giving up their free time, privacy, and social life.

• One-third of the workers have to make career changes to care for elderly relatives: 30 percent have to rearrange their work schedules; 18 percent take time off during the workday; 32 percent have to miss meetings, training seminars, or other educational opportunities; and between 18 percent and 28 percent are forced to take temporary or even permanent leaves of absence.

Noted Scharlach, "What is particularly problematic is that the majority of these employees are in their forties and fifties—people who have been on the job for some time and are among the most loyal, most talented and most important employees a company has. For such employees, temporary or permanent absence from the labor force can have a devastating effect, for employer as well as employee."

Other studies suggest that 20 to 28 percent of employees spend significant time caring for elderly relatives. Almost 10 percent of them report spending at least thirty-five hours a week, as much as a second full-time job.

What these studies don't mention, but is surely a factor, is the point that many women in their forties and fifties are just returning to the work force, so the heavy caretaking burden has the effect of short-circuiting their careers altogether.

Garry Trudeau touched a nerve, albeit humorously, in a "Doonesbury" comic strip that opens with the fiftyish woman lecturing to her mother over the phone. When she hangs up, her husband says, "Have you noticed you've reached an age where you speak to your parents and to your children with almost exactly the same tone of voice?" The thought seems to depress her. She replies, "I don't even want to *think* about what that means." He starts to walk away, saying over his shoulder, "It means don't die. Everyone's counting on you."

Many of us have deeply conflicting feelings about this generational squeeze that places us in the middle between responsibility for our children and responsibility for our aging parents. At a point in our lives when we are able, perhaps for the first time, to spread our wings, we are confronted with a new caretaker role. Our children are replaced by newly needy parents. Of course not every mid-life woman assumes the role of caretaker for her parents. My own parents are self-sufficient and live in another state, and I rarely feel the need to be concerned about them. But as the statistics indicate, it is a common issue for women our age.

During my discussion with the group of women in New Orleans, I asked them to give some thought to what it meant to be the daughters of aging parents.

"I feel that I have so many extra things to worry about now that my parents are getting older," said Mary. "Just in the past year, after my father became ill, I've had a whole new set of concerns. I've never really faced the thought that my parents would someday be unable to physically care for themselves. But last year, suddenly, out of the blue, my father needed triple bypass surgery." Her eyes grew watery. "And I remember thinking, like it was the first time, 'My God, my parents are getting old. I'll probably have to watch them die.' And I wasn't sure I could live through it. On the drive to the hospital my mind kept playing this broken record: 'I can't bear this, I can't bear this.' Oh, and there was something else too. I would never have admitted it, but I didn't really want to go to the hospital at all. I didn't want to see my father in this vulnerable position. I was afraid it would change things between us forever.

"It was like I didn't know how to react or what to do,"

Mary said. "They had always been there for me. I didn't know how to be there for them. At the hospital I could see that my mother had been crying, and I hugged her and knew I had to comfort her and be strong for her. But I was thinking, 'Who is going to comfort me and be strong for me?'. . . oh, that sounds whiny. It isn't quite what I mean."

"Oh, Mary," Sharon chided, "we know what you mean." She turned to me and rolled her eyes. "Mary would rather die than sound dependent, you know. I think those emotions sound perfectly natural. Do any of us really ever get over the feeling that our parents should be there to take care of us forever?"

Angela laughed. "Count me in on that one. My parents live in Arizona now, so I see them only once or twice a year. When you don't see someone regularly, the changes are startling, and lately, I've been shocked by the fact that my parents look old. They never did before. It's disturbing."

"Mortality rears its ugly head," murmured Sharon.

Angela nodded. "Oh, yes. I know what comes at the end of growing old. Dying. I'm like Mary. I doubt my ability to deal with it. Also, things have changed so much, and I hate the change. My parents were always so active, playing tennis, doing things. Now when I visit, we just sit. I feel guilty that I don't enjoy them as much as I used to. I try to get them to come and visit me, but they won't. They want their own pillows, their bed, their bathroom. They hang on to the things they know. I think they're scared—and maybe that's why it's hard to be with them."

"There's another issue too," said Mary. "It's 'What is my responsibility to my parents now?' My father is doing fine, but I feel that I need to help them out more. Maybe, eventually, they should live with me—and I have very mixed feelings about that."

"Which I'm sure make you feel very guilty," teased Sharon.

"Yes, yes, you're right. Part of my feelings have to do with being divorced now. I resent not having another person to share the responsibility with."

"My mother has lived with me for about five years," said Olivia. "I think in the black community we have a different way of relating to extended family. Many people just assume that their parents will live with them at some point. And I think we respect the elderly more. We want our parents to have an influence on our children, and we require that our children respect their elders. It's a shame that our society, in general, doesn't appreciate the elderly."

"I think you're right," I said. "It would be interesting to explore how we lost that sense of the special role of the elderly in this century."

"We're a youth-oriented society," Sharon said.

"My grandmother lived to be ninety-six. She was such a woman!" Olivia's face glowed. "She recited poetry. She had glaucoma, so she memorized it. Respect doesn't even begin to describe the way we felt about her. It was more like awe. My mother is eighty-five. She's quite remarkable, too, and still very lively. Our family has always had a matriarch." She smiled. "I imagine it will be me someday, although I can't imagine how I could hold a candle to these two women."

"Many women our age struggle with being the caretakers of elderly parents," I said. "But I've talked to people who have found creative ways to address this. One woman told of how she and her six siblings shared the responsibility. The mother lives in Oklahoma. Three of the children live in her area, and the others are scattered throughout the country. Each out-of-town child spends two weeks of the year with her. Basically, they handle her care like a business. I don't mean they're cold, just very organized. One of the daughters, who lives nearby, is the primary caretaker. She sends out a newsletter three or four times a year to keep everyone informed. Another person is responsible for the financial affairs, and another handles the upkeep of her home and yard. Because they've worked together to manage the situation, this woman has been able to remain in her home and be independent. It's the greatest gift her children could give to her."

Sharon said, "Five years ago I put my mother in an institution—she's eighty-four and she had Alzheimer's disease. I don't see her much, because she doesn't know who I am. My father died twelve years ago. At first my husband and I took care of my mother—set her up in an apartment near our home and hired caretakers, first part-time, then full-time. But eventually it became impossible. The quality of the care went down, and I was over there all the time. We talked about her coming to live with us, and my husband was completely against it. He had never been close to her, but more than that, it was so clear that she would require full-time care, and I didn't want to become a nursemaid to her. It was like caring for a child. I feel so much better now. She is well cared for, I visit her, and I can continue with my own life. It was a good decision but a difficult one to make."

"What have been your feelings about your mother's deterioration?" I asked.

"Of all the possibilities, this is the worst. My father's death was hard, but at least we had a chance to say good-bye. I'll never have that chance with my mother. Sometimes I tell myself that her soul—her real self—has already gone on to another life. She was always such a sweet, good lady. Now her body is just a shell. I feel as though we're in a state of suspended animation. I want to grieve for her, but I can't, because she's still alive. But she's not really alive." She stared at her hands. "Would everyone be shocked if I said that I wished she would die?"

Mary reached over and rubbed her friend's shoulder in a consoling gesture. "I think we understand exactly what you mean. It's not awful at all."

"It's easier for us to accept the physical deterioration of aging than it is to accept a mental deterioration," I said. "When a person's mind no longer functions, when that person is no longer a unique personality, it calls into question everything we believe about being human. Most people would agree that a person who can no longer function mentally is not human in the same way."

"I've grown to appreciate the argument in favor of euthanasia," said Sharon. "I'm not sure I could do it myself, but I can understand it somewhat. What stops me is that I don't really know for sure what is going on in my mother's mind. She may have a rich mental life that we know nothing about. I hope she does." She dabbed at her eyes with a napkin and smiled weakly. "Has anyone ever noticed how we never escape from being the worriers and fussers? First it's our children; then, by the time they get older and we don't have to take care of them every minute, we're worrying about our parents."

"That's okay, isn't it?" asked Angela. "It's part of what it means to be a family. I'm grateful that I have a family to care about. It would be worse to be alone."

"I don't want to be alone either," said Mary. "But I also don't want to spend the rest of my life being a caretaker and a nurse."

"So, don't do it," Sharon said bluntly. Mary widened her eyes, and Sharon went on. "All our lives we battle with guilt over how much we should give to others and how much we should keep for ourselves. As much as you love your parents, their needs are not more important than yours. You have to find a way to create a balance. A friend of mine told me how she got her husband to help her set limits with her parents' requests for help, because she felt too guilty to say no. I think it's a good idea to enlist the help of your spouse and together develop a plan for how to handle an aging parent."

"It's nice to have permission from a friend," Mary said.

"You're not the only woman in the world who has had to struggle with this issue," I assured her. "If I've discovered one thing in my travels across the country, it is that women share many of the same concerns. It doesn't matter where they live. You should also know that it is perfectly normal and okay to have conflicting feelings about how you relate to your aging parents and how much responsibility you should take for them. Most of us were never prepared for the possibility that we might be responsible for our aging parents on a day-to-day basis. It comes as a shock. It can also be an example of the imbalance in responsibilities we've seen in other areas of our lives. The job of caring for elderly parents falls primarily in the lap of the woman, and this might seem unfair, especially if you are just beginning to experience a freedom from parenting tasks."

"It's a tough subject," said Sharon. "I don't think any of us want to come off sounding like we don't care. We want to be good daughters. But this is a point in our lives when it's hard to know what that means."

❈ ❈

Whether we assume the caretaker role or not, this period in our parents' lives converges with a period of reckoning in our own, and we often go through a reevaluation of their roles in our lives. It is a time of letting go, and one part of the letting-go process involves coming to terms with our relationship with them. During childhood our parents are the central characters in our lives. With early adulthood they take their place on the sidelines. But during our middle years they return to a central position.

"I have a very hard time with it," admitted a woman who cares for her mother, an eighty-nine-year-old woman who lives alone in an apartment nearby. "I do it because it's my duty, but I see her as little as possible. She's always been somewhat critical and humorless, and the tendency has been increasing as she grows older. It's a constant battle to be around her, and she doesn't seem to appreciate anything. If you bring her something, like stockings, she starts a fight with you—'Why did you bring these? They're too long, they're too short, I hate them.'"

I asked the woman how she dealt with her feelings of bitterness. "I try not to be bitter," she said. "I would really like to be able to view this poor old woman with more compassion, because I think she must have had an unhappy life. I'm also learning how *not* to be when I get older. It would be so horrible to think that my children didn't want to be with me or pitied me. One way I've dealt with it is to try to focus on learning from her—in particular, things about family history. And I think I have finally begun to accept the fact that I can't change her and that I can't force her to express her love toward me in the way

I would like her to. I believe she loves me in her own way—the best way she can. Understanding this gives me some peace."

Rhonda, fifty, had been a homemaker nearly all her adult life, and she spoke to me of her feelings of anger about caring for her elderly father. "When my mother died, he began to make demands on me," she told me in frustration. "My daughter is in her twenties now, and he just assumed that I had time on my hands to cater to his every need. He expects me to drive him around and be at his beck and call whenever he wants me. I have a very hard time with this, because all of the excuses I think of sound petty and selfish. How do I say 'Dad, I can't come today because I'm meeting a friend for lunch'? I go back and forth in my mind between thinking I owe him as much attention as he wants because I love him and he might not be around that much longer and resenting him because he makes me feel trapped."

Rhonda admitted that, although she has always been very close to her father, lately she has begun to view him as a burden, and she feels horrified and filled with guilt over her new feelings. In order not to begin resenting her father, Rhonda had to set limits—to do what she could while maintaining her own life. She encouraged him to attend a senior center near his home, and engaged a volunteer who enjoyed walking with him in the neighborhood. Things began to work better once Rhonda had let go of some of the responsibility.

In fact recent studies show that our attitudes toward our parents often become less positive as they grow older. Several years ago the University of Illinois at Chicago developed a Parent Perception Inventory. The goal was to study the changing relationships between mothers and their grown offspring. Many of the study's participants reported that, as they grew more mature, and especially as they had children of their own, they began to see their mothers more as individuals and even as peers. But as the mothers became elderly, their peer status with adult daughters dissolved; the older women were perceived as being less competent and generally were viewed in a more negative light. One suggested reason for this was that the adult children were making a psychological adjustment to an impending loss—an adjustment easier to make by reducing the elderly person's status.

It is also true that elderly parents hold a mirror to our own future. We are forced, through them, to confront our mortality—the inevitability of aging and ultimately death. Sooner than we would like, they will pass the torch to us. It is hard enough to face the death of our parents, who have known us since birth. It is even harder to face the prospect of our own death.

In our aging parents we see the truth, that there will not be enough time to tie up the loose ends before they are gone. We rage against the dying of the light because it seems to occur abruptly, no matter how much preparation we have. Ultimately it seems easier to withdraw before it happens and build a wall against the hurt of our impending loss.

In my years as a psychotherapist I have frequently heard patients mourn the loss of a parent with the words "If only I had told her/him how much she/he meant to me." This is the most common regret expressed after a parent's death. And it is natural to grieve for the words left unspoken and the deeds left undone. We feel guilty that we chose to disengage rather than achieve greater closeness.

Bette Harrell, a forty-six-year-old therapist, considered her feelings about being a parent and daughter and shared with me this piece, which she titled "Legacy—In Tribute and Memory of My Mother":

> I am more experienced at being a child than I am at anything else. I am an expert in being a child. I have been a wife for only twenty years, a therapist for fifteen years, a mother for eighteen years, but I have been a child for forty-six years.
>
> We learn so much from our parents: they teach us how to be men and women, how to be mates, how to be parents, how to be old. We look to them for guidance, for role modeling, for permission to be who we are. The frightening part is that partly who we are is separate from them, different, distinctly us. We often reach a point, or reach

places where we want to go beyond where our parents have gone, where we want more or want differently. Yet to go there means letting go of the old parent/child structure and security; so we are often angry at them, wanting them to change, to go there first, giving us a model, permission, and allowing us to remain the follower, the child. The terror of our aloneness, of our separateness, obscures itself in anger toward them for not being the perfect parent who would thus enable us to be the eternal child.

Separateness and loss are easily confused. So a parent too may want the world for his child and yet fear that his child will grow beyond the platform he has built of his learning, his struggles, his wisdom—the very platform he has built to send his child well equipped into the world. As long as the old order is maintained, that of learned parent and learning child, there is the illusion of oneness, of the impossibility of loss.

The recurring theme of our middle years is one of loss and learning to let go. It is possible for us to move through these years in a constant state of mourning, to let each loss carve an empty space in our heart. It is also possible to embrace change and loss as an ongoing life dynamic, experiences that we build on in the never-ending process of our enrichment.

In her book *Necessary Losses* Judith Viorst pulls a lesson from the sad moments of our good-byes, reminding us that: "We are separate people constrained by the forbidden and the impossible, fashioning our highly imperfect connections. We live by losing and leaving and letting go. And sooner or later, with more or less pain, we all must come to know that loss is indeed 'a lifelong human condition.'"

PARENT AND CHILD: A NEW ROLE

It is natural to have ambivalent feelings toward your parents as you reach mid-life. Nothing in your past has prepared you to face the painful changes that occur. Often it is difficult if you have been close to your parents and have relied on them for emotional and other kinds of support. And it can be even more traumatic to lose a parent from whom you have been alienated. Until he or she dies, there is always the hope that a reconciliation may occur, and death ends that hope. Understanding this, many women who have been alienated from their parents choose to make peace as their parents near the end of life.

But whether or not you feel a closeness to your parents, as they grow older and the roles switch, with you in the position of caretaker, it is almost always a struggle. The psychological leap required is often difficult to negotiate, and you end up feeling abandoned. If your parents were always there to help you through the hard times, you might feel panic-stricken because you have lost your reliable port in the storm. At the same time you wonder how you can provide for them; it does not seem very long ago that you were establishing your independence from them.

Added to the psychological burden is the very real physical role of the caretaker. As we have seen, it is statistically probable that you will in some way be responsible for your elderly parents on a day-to-day basis. Most of the women I spoke with who are in this situation felt horribly guilty about expressing any reluctance to take care of their parents. Deep down, most of them believed that their own needs were frivolous when compared to providing this care. "I had planned for this to be a time for *me*," one woman told me. "But it didn't work out that way. My plans still just have to wait." She said this with a long sigh of sadness. Her face betrayed the belief that her time would never come.

Another woman, whose parents had recently moved in with her and her husband, responded angrily when she heard me speak about how the mid-life period marks the time of new freedom for women. "It isn't true," she challenged me. "I have more responsibilities now than I ever had before." She laughed bitterly. "The only way I would be more free is if I ran away from home. And believe me, I've considered it."

I feel sympathy for women who are challenged by this new responsibility. Talking about it helps. But I also believe that we must begin to structure our own solutions to these issues. Since care for elderly parents has become a common factor, we are called on to look for ways we can make this time a positive one for all concerned. The first step is for us to begin finding ways of realistically evaluating our parents' needs and getting help. Here are some suggestions:

- Investigate services in your community. There are now a growing number of support groups whose task it is to provide education, emotional support, and practical help for adult caregivers. Contact the American Association of Retired Persons, the Older Women's League, the National Organization for Women, or your local hospital or clinic for information.
- If you can afford it, consider utilizing a geriatric management agency. These agencies, which are springing up across the country, charge an hourly fee for the services of trained social workers and caregivers. You can find them through the Yellow Pages, the community health outreach services of local hospitals, or through the offices of M.D.s who specialize in geriatrics.
- Establish a co-op support group in your neighborhood. Find others who are caring for elderly parents and arrange to share services. Or call the Self-Help Clearing House (718-596-6000) to find out about groups that may already exist in your area.
- If you are employed by a large company, approach the management about establishing flexible hours or other means of support for those who are caretakers.
- Encourage your healthy elderly relatives to become involved in organizations and activities designed for them. When they have support groups of their own, your role will become less primary.
- Ask your family for help. Women have a tendency to take on the entire burden by themselves. Involve your husband, children, and other family members.
- Most importantly, don't wait until the situation is critical before you decide what arrangements you are going to make. Every adult child should discuss with her parents the details of their future and make plans for their care.

❋ 7 ❋
In Search of Community

It is a clear spring day in Seattle, the air washed clean by yesterday's rain. I am on my way to visit Susan, a fifty-two-year-old woman who owns her own thriving shop featuring Pacific Northwest artifacts, which she started after her husband died nine years ago. I find Susan's shop on a busy, tightly packed block and look around while she finishes with a customer. Susan clearly enjoys her work; she looks at the same time young and mature, a woman who seems comfortable to be living her midlife years. But later, after we are seated by the window of a popular waterfront restaurant close to her shop and have ordered lunch, Susan admits to me that she is terrified about getting older, particularly about being alone in her later years.

"Starting a business was such a major thing in my life," she says. "Once I got over the grief of losing Doug, I became excited about starting over and doing something on my own. But I've aged so much in the past few years—not in the way I feel but in my looks."

"You don't look old to me," I tell her honestly.

She laughs sharply. "Oh, but you aren't a man who is evaluating my worthiness for a relationship—not to mention a date. In so many ways my life has been good since Doug died. I love my work, I have friends, my children have turned into wonderful adults.

"But sometimes I feel so bitter that this man who adored me died. I feel like, God, what's happened to me? Here I am, this person—smart, independent, basically happy. But I have no one. And I'm getting older and older. I have hard feelings about not having someone to love who also loves me. I really looked forward to growing old with my husband. I thought it would be so cozy and wonderful—like a peaceful scene from a movie where the sun sets gently over the horizon. Wasn't this what it was all about? Hadn't I earned that chance after all the years of struggle and hard work? I guess I felt that I had those years coming to me, so when Doug died I thought I had been cheated. Now I don't know what it will be like to grow old. I don't have a picture anymore."

"Everyone is afraid of being alone in later life," I observe gently. "In a way you're describing a different kind of biological clock, aren't you? Get a man before you are too old to attract one. It's a hard place to be."

"There were two men after Doug died," she tells me. "Neither of the relationships lasted very long. Looking back, I can see that I was trying too hard, I was too obsessed with the idea of having someone and too afraid that something would go wrong. I think my neediness drove them away.

"Now I'm involved again, and have been for six months, but he's married, so it's a pretty imperfect situation."

I nod. She looks very vulnerable, and I am struck, as I have been so many times before, with the uncanny ways that the fears of adolescence are so often mirrored in the eyes of older women.

"Where's it headed?" She shrugs. "God knows. I'm not depressed about having a part-time man. It's *almost* okay—but it isn't really okay, if you know what I mean. I keep trying to think of a way to make it okay in my head because I think he would have been Mr. Right for me if it weren't for his being married. I'm always thinking I'll end it, but he might be the last man in my life, so I'm scared to let go of him."

She sets down her fork and takes a sip of wine, considering. "It's very complicated," she says finally. "For one thing, men seem to be interested only in the younger women. I've met a lot of men since Doug died, and it's just as bad as everyone says. They're the same type—uncommitted, unavailable men. Of course I've read all the books—women who love men who hate women, etc.—but when you finish those books, you're just left with the feeling that it's somehow all your fault. After a while you begin to think, 'It's me. I'm neurotic. I'd be able to have a good relationship if I wasn't so messed up.' It makes me crazy, angry."

I shrug. "Why wouldn't it? Too many women are walking around with a burden on their shoulders, thinking if only they themselves could be better they'd be able to have a man, any man."

"Right. And half the time I don't even like the men I meet. But I think, 'You're getting old, you can't be so choosy.' I'm really mad that I don't have a man and that I feel too old to get one.

"I think about it a lot, I'm really trying to come to terms with the idea of being alone. I try to make it seem okay. Like, is it okay to have a part-time man and be happy only part of the time? Sometimes I wonder why I let the idea of having a man or not having a man interfere with my idea of happiness at all. No great answers there."

"What's it like with this man?"

She sighs. "Oh, I guess I could say he makes me happy in a momentary kind of way. But I wish I could have more faith."

"Faith . . . meaning?"

"Faith that he won't leave me—no." Susan shakes her head. "It isn't even that. Faith that I won't fall apart if he does. Faith in me first."

She picks up her fork again, and we go on eating. I am thinking about sitting across the table from a lovely, successful, intuitive woman of fifty-two, whose life seems to her unaccountably hollow. "If only we could live without this fear." I speak suddenly, not knowing I'm going to say it. "I'm married, but these fears don't all simply dissolve because a man is around. How is it, I wonder, that women like ourselves who are filled with life and energy and possibility can speak with such bleak resignation about our lives as though they were already over? You and I—we're healthy. We could live another thirty years. Are those years less meaningful somehow without a man? I don't think so."

She listens quietly while I say my piece, then shakes her head slowly. "No . . . no, they're not. I feel as though I've been given a whole second life with my business. I love it. In my truly honest moments I would never suggest that it is less meaningful than the years I shared with my husband—just different. But these victories are less fun when they can't be shared. Does it make me weak to want support and sharing and a person in my life who cares about me first?"

- -

Susan wasn't weak—far from it. Her fears were normal, and she was coping with them as well as she knew how. Being alone is a very large part of the experience of growing older for many women, and it is perhaps the most challenging issue of this book for me. Why? Because I had known the same fear myself before I met my current husband, and sometimes even know it now, since life is never guaranteed. Because I had met so many women in this age group who were living alone and very few who had made peace with it. Because I knew that, given the statistics, it was more likely than not that most of us would find ourselves at some point alone in our later years. I recognized that we share a challenge: to move beyond the paralysis of loneliness and reinvent the forms of solidarity that will support us until the end of our lives.

I hear so many women of my age crying the sad Peggy Lee refrain: "Is that all there is?" If women like Susan feel cheated by the disappearance of the one they loved, many other women feel left out altogether, because although they had wanted to be married, they hadn't found the right partner. They are, in many cases, the very women who have fulfilled the dreams of our new era, going out and pioneering new professional opportunities. They made the clear choice to marry later, when their careers were built, but found themselves looking up in their forties to find that maybe they had lost the chance. They are smart, attractive, wonderful women who admit that they feel stranded.

The writer Molly Haskell struck a chord of recognition when she wrote in the *New York Times Magazine* about the never-married woman of a certain age. She recalled the childhood game of Old Maid, which she had played in the 1950s, noting the dreadful significance of holding the feared spinster card. "Like *witch, spinster* was a scare word," wrote Haskell, "a stereotype that served to embrace and isolate a group of women of vastly different dispositions, talents, situations, but whose common bond—never having become half of a pair—was enough to throw into question the rules and priorities on which society was founded."

The image of spinster has stayed in our consciousness, even in more enlightened times. It is still assumed that an unmarried man has *chosen* his status, while an unmarried woman is there because she has not been chosen. Of course many women have chosen not to be married or, at least, not to be married to any man who they've met so far. But in spite of their independency, there has been the sense of being lost, of not belonging to the larger circle of society. The circle does not include them so easily. "Our world operates in twos," one woman observed. "People never quite know what to do with a woman who is alone. Sometimes my married friends seem to be almost embarrassed by me. They grow impatient, as though they're thinking 'Why doesn't she find a man so she'll fit in better?'"

Recalling the conversations I had with mid-life women about their childhood role models, I realized that they often mentioned unmarried women who, in their young eyes, seemed different and glamorous, not trapped in normalcy like their own mothers. They mentioned a favorite writer, who wrote vividly of the adventures experienced in her world travels, an unmarried aunt who had boyfriends (after their own parents had ceased to seem like lovers), a nun wrapped in the mystery of her vocation who moved with authority and dignity. "My grandmother was alone from the time she was forty-five," one woman told me. "Everyone thought she became a little eccentric after my grandfather's death, but not me! She was so neat. She lived in this little house a mile away from us, and her garden was my escape. She treated me with respect and told me wild stories from her youth and took me shopping downtown. I envied her. I remember wondering how anyone could want to be married and be tied down to a boring life when she could live like this."

It is ironic that we ourselves are afraid to be like the ones we admired. And a further irony is that the single women today, who have the opportunity to live lives far more glamorous and free than those of our youth, have no doubt become the role models for a whole new generation of young women. And they don't even know it.

There is a sense, too, among women who are not married that their lives are not taken as seriously, that their time is not as valuable. "I have six brothers and sisters, but almost all of the care of our elderly mother falls to me," one woman told me. "Everyone else in the family has the attitude that 'We have our own families to take care of, and you have no one, so you should do it.' I am treated by them as a person with no valid needs of my own."

※- -※

Betty, forty-eight, has never been married. She might be the perfect symbol for where a woman of her age should be—except that she feels lonely. Her beloved dog, George, her companion of sixteen years, was recently put to sleep. "It might sound crazy to some people," she tells me when I visit, "but without George I feel that I have no one to lean on. When George was put to sleep, it was an exquisite moment of realizing that I am all alone.

"I feel that being unmarried is stereotyped in a negative

way," she says. "I can think of only two or three times when it hasn't been an issue for people to invite me someplace as a single person. Otherwise it's a two-by-two world, and most of the time I feel that I don't fit in. For example, when my friends have a party, they expect me to bring someone. It makes them uncomfortable if I don't. There's one man, in particular, who is a very good friend, and he's gay. He's not in a relationship now, so it makes sense for us to go out together. I realize it's a deception, since my friends don't know he's gay, and I have to ask myself, and I *have* asked myself, what this deception is all about. Why should I feel ashamed not to have a man in my life? But you have to admit, there's a stigma. My gay friend is very handsome, and I know it makes me look good to be with him. I hate everything that this deception implies, but that's just the way it is."

She stops talking and stares reflectively out the window. "The past few years I've organized my life around taking care of George, my dog. It has been a very strong attachment. Now that he's gone, it will be interesting to see whether this will change my ideas about being alone—whether I'll think about adopting a child or look more aggressively for a man.

"You know"—she smiles, tugging her hair back into the clip—"I've always been so independent. I just knew when I was young that I wasn't going to get married right away and be tied down like so many women I knew. I used to admire the nuns who taught in my school. They seemed to lead more independent, interesting lives than the woman who stayed home with a bunch of kids. I wouldn't change what I've accomplished. I don't regret it. But the issue does become more important as I grow older."

Betty unfolds her legs and pulls herself up in the chair. "I want to make sure that I don't leave you with the wrong impression," she says seriously. "On the face of it, it might sound as though my life is full of worry and loneliness, but that's not accurate. These fears I've expressed are real, but they don't consume me. Far from it. Generally I like my life. I'm proud of what I've accomplished, and I am lucky to have many good friends. When I look back to the emotional roller coaster I rode during my twenties and thirties, I have to conclude that this is the most secure time of my life. It's not perfect—but who can really say their lives are perfect? Overall, things are good for me. I'm not complaining."

Women like Betty might sometimes feel as though they are outside the norm, but the reverse is true. And as we grow older, the number of single women increases substantially. The National Center for Health Statistics reports that in 1990 there are two million more women than men who are aged sixty-five to seventy-five. It's a fact that most of us are aware of, even if we are living with healthy men. The statistics are clear: married or not, most women will find themselves at some point in their later years without a man. Sometimes it seems, as I talk with women, that it is one of those facts that we *know* yet refuse to know. None of us wants to face the inevitabilities of aging, least of all the possibility that we will live out our final years in loneliness. In the many conversations I have had with women, I have watched them take the tentative steps toward planning a future without a man. Repeatedly women express embarrassment about how strongly they fear this inevitability, as though, in this day and age, women should be able to stand alone and be stronger.

I have heard many of them talk about man-sharing, an idea that once might have been unthinkable, or planning a future with their female friends. There is a sense that options exist if one can be open to them.

I've come to realize that it is not simply the absence of a man that is the point of struggle, although that absence is the one most often articulated. As one woman explained, "I don't want to be married. Ever since I broke up with the man I lived with for ten years, I have loved being on my own, and I would prefer not to live with another person. Where I struggle is with the deeper notion of community—the need to have people around me who share my vision of life ... people I can be close to. I believe that humans need to be together, and although we have reduced this need to marriage, it is far more than being married. Sadly, we don't know how to develop communities that are outside the norm, which is why those of us who are unmarried feel that we have no community. Lately I've been realizing that it is within my power to create my own extended family of important people. For example, I love to read, and recently I advertised for people interested in forming a study group to read certain books and meet once a week to talk about them."

Another woman articulated a similar view. "I was feeling sorry for myself, but I couldn't quite put my finger on what was wrong. I was the one who decided to end the marriage, so it wasn't as though I felt abandoned. I think it was mostly that I was restless and bored. Then, a couple of years ago, I heard about this organization called International Peace Walk, which was groups of people from all over the world walking in the U.S.S.R., Eastern Europe, and China. I remember feeling a deep excitement in the pit of my stomach that I had not felt for a long time. This was it! So I went on a peace walk last fall, and I can honestly say that it changed my life. It's hard to describe the feeling of awe when you recognize that you fit into the human community and play a part in its development. I no longer think of myself as a lonely, isolated person in a big world. The world has become small enough that I can reach out and touch people in every corner."

I saw this point most clearly expressed in my conversation with a fifty-year-old nun who, although she had chosen a life without a married partnership with a man, found herself in committed partnerships with many people, both male and female. In fact her whole life was built on the joint concepts of community and making a contribution to the world. Perhaps because her attention was focused away from the typical concerns that women have as they grow older, she had little fear of the future. In her community prestige increased rather than declined with age. Her circle of close friends and colleagues, as well as her sense of achievement, expanded with the years, and she was hard-pressed to name any barriers to future fulfillment.

※- -※

"Unmarried women are the pathfinders for the rest of us," Janice observed several months after she buried her husband.

"They have a lot to teach us about the kind of living most of us will be doing." When she said this, Janice had already moved beyond her rage over her husband's leaving her "in the lurch" at the relatively young age of forty-nine. The edge was off her sorrow, and now she was experiencing a somewhat numbed state of resignation.

Janice had been referred to me as a patient shortly after her husband died suddenly of a heart attack; he was only fifty-four. She had initially been resistant to therapy. "There's nothing wrong with me that time won't cure," she said the first time she sat across from me in the sunny upstairs room I had converted into an office. Nevertheless, despite her reservations she stayed, and eventually she seemed to look forward to our time together and, I hope, was helped by it.

Janice had no children, and during our sessions she talked a lot about being alone and the many fears that her new single state brought to the surface. Sometimes she would ache with the loss of the man she had loved and lived with for almost her entire adult life. At other times she would outline the terrifying specifics of her aloneness. "What if something happened to me?" she would ask, her eyes widening at the thought. "What if I got sick? My parents are dead, and I have no children. I have a sister who lives in Pennsylvania, but she has her own family to worry about. So do my friends..." Her voice tightened in panic.

In the early days Janice fought against hearing words of encouragement, not wanting to acknowledge new possibilities for her future until she was ready to let go of her deep grief. Eventually, as her sense of resignation grew, she started trying to cope with a future alone.

"Why are you so set on the idea that you'll be alone?" I asked her once. She shrugged. "Right now I can't even think about getting married again, and even if I wanted to, you know the chances aren't very good for a woman of my age."

"There are other ways of not being alone," I said. "Your friends..."

She nodded slowly, her eyes lighting up a little. "Yes, that's something I've started thinking more about. I know I talk about being alone—we all do—as though it's inevitable and I'll just have to get used to it, but in my heart of hearts is just doesn't make any sense." She looked at me questioningly. "Does it?"

I motioned for her to continue.

"There are so many people who are alone, especially women at this age. I read the statistics. But we're only thinking about being together in a very narrow way. The way things are now, my best friend in the world could live down the block in a big house all by herself, and I could live in my big house all by myself, and we could both complain about being alone, but it would never occur to us to get together."

"That's a good point," I said, feeling very interested in what she was saying. "I read recently that in California alone almost a quarter of a million people, a large percentage of them older, live by themselves in houses with three or more bedrooms."

She smiled suddenly, brightly. "Actually I've had an idea, like a fantasy. There are five of us women, and every year we go hiking in the woods together and stay at a mountain retreat. It's very nice. And my fantasy is that when we're older we'll get together and buy a big property, maybe somewhere in the mountains. And we'll build cottages—each of us will have our own—plus a larger communal area. There will be privacy, so we can entertain our friends privately or do whatever we want to do. But we'll be together, too, when we want to be. Our holiday celebrations will be big family-style events. And maybe we'll travel together. It's a little crazy, but I like to think that something like that is possible."

I was pleased to see Janice looking so animated. "I don't think your fantasy is crazy at all. It sounds wonderful. Have you talked with the others about this?"

"We did talk about it a little a couple of years ago. I didn't go last year, because it was right after Gary died. I don't think any of us took the idea seriously, but we had a lot of fun imagining it. It became like a game. Each person would think of something different to add."

"I've been talking to a lot of women our age around the

country, and you'd be surprised to hear how many have similar thoughts. And whenever I mention it to the other women, there's always a lot of enthusiasm. For many people communal living makes more sense than being alone." As I said this, I was thinking of an experience I had had that showed how well a communal style can work. When my children were young and I was teaching college, the mothers organized a baby-sitting co-op, a co-op nursery school, and other shared arrangements. I wonder sometimes how we might bring the idea of a collective into a plan for our later years.

"I think that some people, if you mention this idea about communities of women," Janice said, "would figure that you're just making do under the circumstances—as opposed to living in a way that you really want to live. Have you seen the movie *Steel Magnolias?*" I nodded. "Those women had such a good time together. And they were so supportive of each other. There were men around, and they seemed nice and solid, but they weren't really interesting. You ask anyone, and I'm sure they'd tell you that, given a choice, they'd much rather be with the women. The point is, living in a community of women in our later years can be seen as a very enriching lifestyle, not just a way of making do."

※- -※

Maggie Scarf, a Connecticut science and medical writer who has studied depression in women, observed that "Emotional attachments are much more important to women than men, and women find the idea of ending a relationship—even a very bad relationship—to be monstrous. They think, 'Who or what would I be if I were alone?' They feel horrified at the thought of being alone. Sometimes they would rather commit suicide than be alone." For this reason, it's a good idea to experiment with being alone—even when you're married. For example, it's good occasionally to take a trip by yourself. You'll learn things, and it may help you feel stronger.

I think it is not because women are weak that they fear the lonely state. It is a far more complex matter than that. Being alone should not be viewed as a sad plight or a test of strength. Our failing as a society is that we have not found ways to enable people to come together in different and creative ways. We have put all of our eggs in one basket; it is the basket of love and marriage. We have idealized this state to the extent that people naturally feel inadequate when they have not achieved it or when they, through divorce or death, lose hold of it.

The mid-life woman who finds herself divorced after a long marriage can rightfully feel that all the decks are stacked against her. Not only does divorce take an emotional toll; it takes an economic one as well. A recent study of divorce in California revealed that the standard of living for women declined 73 percent within the first year after divorce. Men, on the other hand, experienced a 42 percent increase. For women whose husbands were the primary breadwinners, special complications often emerged during the negotiation of divorce settlements, such as their rights to a portion of his pension or the continuation of health insurance. Until recently, when several states passed legislation that includes the husband's pension as marital property upon divorce, many women faced the prospect of growing old in poverty. It's a scary thing to look ahead into one's later years and be uncertain that the money will be there. In their darkest moments many of these women admit that they can envision themselves joining the growing ranks of the elderly homeless.

Feeling assaulted by jarring truths and awesome losses, it might be tempting for these women to curl into themselves and wait for the doom to roll in like a fatal wave. "It is a common illusion," writes Louise Bernikow in *Alone in America*, "that the presence of another person will protect us from death.... Many people have spoken to me about the connection between loneliness and fear and dying. Loneliness does feel, at times, like death, the death, at least, of a part of oneself. But the fear spoken more often is quite literal—alone, unprotected by another person, I could easily die."

But there is another side to being alone. Some women, when they get past the fragile early days of divorce or widowhood, are struck with a revelation that comes to them like a deep curiosity and the sense that an unknown adventure awaits them. While they once believed that surprise and creation were the domains of the young, they now find themselves asking again, as they did when they were twenty, "Who am I?" In these moments failure and fear are transformed, the cloak of victimhood is dropped, and they are able to let go of the negative beliefs that no longer have a place in their lives.

"When I told my children that I planned to spend the Christmas holidays alone at a bed-and-breakfast in Maine, they tried hard to talk me out of it," said Jackie, fifty-four years old, who had been divorced in the spring of that year. "In their minds this was the last thing in the world I should do. They wanted to surround me with people and the warmth of their celebration, and I loved them for that. But I had been thinking for a while that the time had come for me to find a new way to be. I was so tired of being sad, of struggling with demons in the night, of wishing my life had not turned out the way it had. I wanted to be free from all of that, and I realized the answer had to be found inside, not outside.

"Until my divorce I had never spent any real time alone during my adult life, having moved from my parents' home directly into marriage. I felt that I still had a lot to learn about myself, and it seemed very urgent that I not put off the process any longer. Once I decided to go, I made a pact with myself that I would not allow myself, during this trip, the luxury of despair over my failed marriage or a time to recount all that I might have been. I put a positive spin on the experience. It would be like a religious retreat. I would ask myself questions, write in my journal, soak up the atmosphere, explore the area, have fun.

"I have one special memory from that trip. On Christmas Eve, in the late afternoon, I went for a walk along a tree-lined road outside the inn. There was snow on the ground, and it was slow going. I made new footprints on the untraveled road with my big rubber boots. Everything was so quiet, and I realized I loved the silence, that the scene would be ruined by the voice of another person. That was the point when I really came to terms with the fact that I was okay—even great—alone and that there were times to be alone and times to be together, and I could live happily with both."

※ ※

Cheryl likes to tell the story about how her boyfriend came to her door wrapped in a red ribbon on her fiftieth birthday. "I'm your birthday present," the handsome forty-four-year-old man told her.

"I was feeling chipper that day," she remembers three years later. "I had just met this great new guy, and was feeling good about myself."

Today Cheryl has come a long way from that point. She still looks and feels great, but her wonderful "birthday present" is a thing of the past, and she admits that it has been a hard adjustment.

"I never for a minute thought I would marry him," she says, shaking her short blond curls for emphasis. She tells me about her experiences with the man she loved, an alcoholic who led her into a dark world.

"I had never had any experience with the disease before, and I guess I was very naive. I felt like I was the one who was out of control, as though I was addicted to him."

"That's a common pattern for women involved with alcoholics," I tell her.

"Yes." She grimaces. "I know that now. But for a long time I let it go, hoping things would settle down once we grew more comfortable with each other. I was the one who called it quits, but it was hard. Even now I sometimes get this tremendous urge to call him. And when that happens, here's what I do." She leads me into the kitchen and shows me a list that she has taped to her refrigerator. "These are his traits," she says, reading the list aloud. "Inappropriate behavior, out of touch with reality, crisis-oriented, poor impulse control, self-destructive, gender identity confusion, suicidal, sociopathic behavior." Cheryl turns and leans against the refrigerator, smiling sadly. "You'd think I would have run from him as though he were the plague. But I broke up with him and went back to him twice. Six weeks ago I broke up with him a third time, and this time I'm determined to make it stick."

"I know it isn't easy," I sympathize. "As bad as these men's behavior seems to be, there are always compelling things about them that make you want to stay."

"Oh, yes," Cheryl agrees. "Greg had so many great things about him—or let's say I chose to look at him through rose-colored glasses. He was a genius artistically, and I admired that. And when he wasn't being difficult, he was so attentive, taking care of me, helping around the house, cooking great romantic meals. It was all so seductive. I kept thinking 'I'm so lucky to have this at fifty years old.' But I know that a lot of it was manipulation on his part." She sighs. "I tell you, it's like a divorce, this breakup. And it's harder now because I'm fifty-three years old."

After I met Cheryl, I spent a lot of time thinking about why women allow themselves to get caught up in relationships with inappropriate and abusive partners. Of course this happens at every age, but it seems possible that as women get older they are more vulnerable. I think about Cheryl's long struggle with an alcoholic man, a struggle she could not win . . . of Susan confiding to me how hard she tries to make her clearly inadequate relationship with a married man "okay" in her mind. At the same time, there were other women, like Jackie, who were consciously working to get beyond their fears and to create a new paradigm of the woman of their age. Having named their fear, they aimed more boldly toward rising above the initial panic of being alone and struggled to identify themselves as whole without another.

Societal norms encourage women to fit their dreams into the framework of marriage or coupledom. But, in fact, our dreams spill out into so many other arenas. The truth (and such a hard truth for people to believe!) is that many women living alone focus very little on the idea of marriage. Other goals take center stage, and self-worth and personal pride are found in their fulfillment. I think of Eleanor, the fifty-one-year-old domestic who had only a third-grade education. She had divorced young and been solely responsible for raising her four children. But now that they're adults, Eleanor has set out to fulfill her long-held dreams. She is studying for a high school equivalency degree, saving her money, and thinking about traveling. Last year Eleanor purchased a small piece of property in Florida, and she looks forward to moving there permanently sometime in the next ten years. She speaks with pride and a deeply felt satisfaction that she is now living the life she always dreamed about.

It is a curious thing that, although the entire fabric of the American family is far different from what it was thirty years ago, as a society we maintain a determined nostalgia for the time before things began to change. As a consequence we have faced poorly or not at all the demands of this change. There has been much talk about the so-called crisis in the American family, but we are at best vague about what this crisis might be. It seems clear that one aspect of the crisis is that we have, during the past thirty or forty years, created millions of separate nuclear units (often in the newfound isolation of suburbia) that are self-contained and self-sufficient. And gradually, as things have changed, family members have split apart from the nucleus and there has been a fragmentation for a variety of reasons. For one thing, people are moving more; they are less likely than previous generations to live all their lives in the communities of their youth. More people are divorcing; almost ten million men and women are raising their children as single parents. Nearly 70 percent of all women work outside the home, and people are having fewer children. And thanks to a combination of advances in medical technology and better health practices, we are living longer and there is a whole new community of senior citizens that literally did not exist in previous times. As Ken Dychtwald observed in *Age Wave*, "the nuclear family, which fulfilled a unique function, was one of the shortest-lived family metamorphoses in history. According to Dr. Matilda White Riley, president of the American Sociological Association, 'As four (or even five) generations of many families are now alive at the same time, we can no longer concentrate primary attention on nuclear families of young parents and their children.'"

Most of the women I have met feel more isolated than they expected to feel by the time they were fifty. Even those who have husbands and children find the security of their family's embrace less absolute than they once believed it to be. Concern runs deepest among women who have not developed independent careers. They are more inclined to wonder what might happen if they were on their own. Could they make ends meet? I was surprised to find how many women our age have fears about becoming homeless. It was once an unthinkable fate, but the woman who lives in an apartment and struggles to make ends meet might be only one rent payment away from her sister on the street. In fact those who work in shelters for the homeless have noticed a substantial increase in the numbers of women over sixty-five. One administrator told me, "It's scandalous. These aren't crazy ladies. They are respectable, formerly middle-class women whose savings went down the drain caring for sick husbands, or who don't have pensions, or who couldn't find jobs. Many of them are widows. It's very hard to face that we have not provided a safety net for these women. Where's the humanity? Those who preach about the need to return to family values should ask themselves what is more central to any value system than the instinct to help one's neighbor and the compassion to embrace those who find themselves on the outside."

※ ※

When asked by an interviewer from *Lear's* magazine how she related to the fact that an ever-increasing number of women over the age of fifty were living alone, without men, Betty Friedan, the longtime (and often strident) spokesperson for the feminist movement, denied that this fact indicated a lack of desirability or that these women lived sterile, loveless lives. "I'm not sure that lack of love is the issue," said Friedan. "For instance, there's an awful lot of love in my life, if I think about it. The first thing I did after I divorced was to start a 'commune' of women and men who were in various states of non-marriage. By sharing a big house weekends and summers, we gave one another a new kind of family."

Of course Friedan's use of the word *commune* might scare some. But I have heard women describe, in dozens of different ways, a similar eagerness to experiment, in their middle and later years, with a new way of being family. Many of these are women who have, unlike Friedan, lived very conventional lives. Their new ideas about creating different kinds of community have evolved from their experiences; they do not consider themselves radicals. Even Friedan acknowledges that it is not a particularly radical idea that people, as they age, should ask for community in a different configuration from the one that served them in their younger years. "There should be much more provision for the pooling of resources and mutual support," she said, "and it need not be based on sexual union or family ties. We really need new forms of family and of intimacy. People need to feel part of a community."

These new concepts of community do not ignore the importance of sexuality or the role of romance. When women have shared with me their ideas about creating communities of older women, their point has never been to negate their sexuality (or, rather, their heterosexuality). Instead they have said that women who do not have partners (meaning husbands) should not have less value and, on a larger scale, that these communities might help to reinvent family as a structure of love and support that brings strangers together and binds them within the larger human community.

The French writer Françoise Sagan once observed about family life, "I think it is always possible to achieve it from the instant people have the time to love one another and room in which to express it without bumping into one another or being obsessive. But family life may be life with one's friends or life among centenarians, just as certain lives shared with members of a true family can be living hell. It depends on the individuals." As Sagan suggests, the dynamic of being family transcends the limited ways we have often chosen to express it.

There is a picture I keep in my mind about a group of women who live the way I think I would like to live someday. I've never met these women; I refer to them always as "the four o'clock ladies' swim." I was introduced to them by my friend Katharine, who is fifty-three. Katharine lives with her second husband in a big house not far from my own, and she is very involved in the lives of her children and stepchildren. We were talking one day last year, sitting on the glassed-in porch that faces the back of Katharine's house. Not unexpectedly, the conversation turned to the issues addressed in this book and to our own feelings about this precarious age. Katharine is beautiful and young-looking, with rich dark hair, so I laughed when she said "I always assumed that when I turned fifty I would be blue-haired and sitting in tearooms."

"Wearing a shawl and a blanket over your legs," I teased.

"Right. I don't feel that I've changed that much since I turned fifty, except in little ways. My skin isn't as resilient, and I gain weight more easily. I feel flabby in a bathing suit—things like that. But Lee still flatters me, so I'm not really bothered by it.

"The one thing I noticed when I reached fifty was that my perception of myself as a woman changed. Before, I thought of myself as someone men would be interested in, but suddenly I didn't see myself that way any longer. And you know what? It didn't depress me in the least. In fact it was a great relief. I thought, 'Oh, good, I don't have to worry about that anymore.'"

Even though Katharine was happily married, she admitted that she sometimes thought about preparing herself for a time when she would be alone. The women in her family had traditionally lived many years longer than their husbands, and she suspected that she would too. I asked her if she had a picture in her mind of what that time would be like for her.

She smiled in a dreamy way. "Did I ever tell you about the four o'clock ladies' swim?"

I shook my head.

"There's this woman who is a few years older than I, and

we've known each other ever since I can remember. Our grandmothers were friends. Every summer she and her sister spend their vacations together at the Cape [Cape Cod], and they've done this for years. Anyway, a few years back they instituted something called the four o'clock ladies' swim. It's just a group of women in their fifties and sixties. No youngsters allowed." Katharine grinned. "They probably wouldn't even let you in since you're not fifty yet. Every afternoon they meet at four o'clock and swim and talk for a couple of hours, as they breaststroke across the bay. Doesn't it sound like a nice thing to do?"

"I love it," I said.

"You can just imagine all the things they must talk about. Anyway, she told me that they've decided that they all want to live together when they get old—by which they mean in their seventies and eighties. It's a neat idea. It really inspired me to hear about it, because suddenly I realized that maybe growing old doesn't have to mean being alone. Maybe it could mean something different from anything I've ever thought about before. Now I have a picture of us—you and me and my other friends—as eighty-year-old women, living in the same area and meeting every afternoon for a swim and a talk. It's a comforting picture, a nice picture. When I think of it in this way, growing older doesn't seem so scary anymore."

❋ ❋

When she turned fifty, Frances bought a small house with two female friends and a male friend in a rural community near Chesapeake Bay. It is the first property Frances has ever owned. She has spent most of her adult years in a rented apartment in Philadelphia's Center City.

She has invited me to visit on a summer weekend, and when I arrive after a long drive I see her settled in the garden in front of a small white house, dressed in baggy shorts and a T-shirt, happily pulling up weeds. She greets me with a hug and leads me inside, where the house is cooled by large ceiling fans. Frances is alone in the house this weekend, and there is a comfortable quiet that lingers in the small rooms. We take big glasses of lemonade out onto the screened porch and sit down to talk. The porch looks out onto the road, and often during our conversation neighbors pass by and wave or call out hellos.

"I like this," Frances says, her sun-reddened face shining with enthusiasm. "I've lived in the city for my entire adult life, and it's the first time I've experienced this feeling of being part of my community. I know everyone in this town."

Frances was married once for six years, when she was in her twenties. In the intervening years she has had two serious relationships, but neither has led to marriage. She has no children.

"The year I turned forty, I decided I'd better get busy and find a permanent relationship," she says. "The clock was ticking away—it was now or never. I joined a singles group and spent a lot of time working on finding a man. But that experience taught me some important things I hadn't realized about myself. First, that I wasn't so eager to have a man around that I would settle for any man. I went out with dozens of men, and some of them were very interested in me. But I wasn't interested in them, so it wasn't good enough. The second thing I realized was that I had grown very independent. I wasn't about to give that up for another person. I suddenly wasn't sure that I wanted to live with someone all the time.

"These realizations made me feel better about myself, stronger. I stopped looking so desperately for a man and started concentrating on cultivating a strong circle of friends that included both men and women. I made an effort to renew old friendships, and I made new ones. I didn't have a family, and I thought, 'That's what I need.'" She leans toward me excitedly, and the old porch chair squeaks. "We are not victims. It isn't a matter of 'poor me, I'm all alone.' People who are alone are that way by choice. If you want to be with other people, to have a community or family, you have the choice to do that."

I feel that her point was a great revelation. "What I hear you saying is that the reason so many women are stuck in this lonely place is that they see only one way to be committed, and that is as part of a traditional couple."

"Exactly. And that point of view demeans us. It is also unrealistic, because as we grow older there are fewer men available. I don't want to be involved in this mad scramble to land the few remaining men." She laughs, amused at the thought. "It's stopped having meaning for me. It's boring. I have so much more fun now. I teach during the year and spend the summers down here, and I have neighbors and friends, and there are always people around. In fact, tonight I'm taking you to a big crab bake down the road. It will be a lot of fun."

"Great." I lean against the back of the chair and sip my lemonade. "This place is contagious, Frances. I feel so relaxed here. How did you find this wonderful house?"

"My friends Amy, John, and Ruth, and I all live in the city, and we started talking about it two summers ago. We're very good friends, all in our early fifties, and we decided that we were letting our lives slip by. John and Amy are both divorced, and Ruth has never been married. Amy's parents used to have a place down here, and it was her idea to look in this area. We found this old house and bought it for an amazingly low price. Of course it needed a lot of work, but that was part of the fun of it. Ruth and I are both teachers, so we live here full-time during the summer. Amy and John come on weekends, and we all come down on various weekends during the winter. We had central heating installed. Last winter we decided to hold a country Thanksgiving dinner here. We invited ten other people, and it was picture-perfect. It didn't snow—we're too close to the bay—but everything else about it was ideal. It's what I mean when I talk about creating a family. I feel that we've done that. None of us will ever be alone, because we have each other."

"It seems that you have accomplished something important here," I say. "It's like you've discovered a great secret—but really it's not such a secret. It's there for everyone to see. I've talked to many single, divorced, and widowed women who feel absolutely panicked, but your solution is available to them as well."

"Right. It sounds trite to say it, but once I stopped desperately looking for a man who would assure that I wouldn't be lonely in my later years, I started actually meeting men—and women—who gave me what I had been looking for. It's like the old D. H. Lawrence poem that I heard many years ago and has stayed with me." She pauses, collecting the words in her head. "It goes, 'Those who go searching for love only make manifest their own lovelessness. And the loveless never find love. Only the loving find love, and they never have to search for it.'" She grins, a little embarrassed, and stands up. "Listen to me, reciting poetry. This place does that. But now it's time to get back to reality. The men have caught twelve bushels of crabs this morning, and we've got to get ready for the big feed. Wear your old clothes. It's a messy business, eating crabs with twenty people."

THE FAMILY OF THE FUTURE

I found the discovery of new community styles to be an instructive and exhilarating aspect of my research. It demonstrated to me that many times we are sending women the wrong message when we say "Learn to love yourself and you won't need a partner." In fact all of us need "significant others" in our lives—it is an essential part of being human. The problem is that we have not, as a society, invented the new ways of being family and community that address the demographic realities.

The hopeful word is that, whether you are married or single, there are possibilities for you to extend your family, to have people you can count on and who count on you. The outdated nuclear family ideal is no longer the norm, and it isn't necessarily the ideal.

I also discovered that, as we reach this point in our lives, women move naturally to form closer relationships with their female friends. Countless women told me that they expect to spend their later years in some form of women's community, and it is not surprising that we would finally look to one another for the most meaningful forms of support. With women outliving men in substantial numbers, it makes sense that we would find in other women the lasting support that we have learned to expect from our families.

❦ 8 ❦
A Celebration of Fifty

I call turning fifty a second coming of age because it involves many of the same impulses and emotions that were present in our youth. We feel the urgency once again, the curiosity, and the desire to test our limits.

I remember a feeling I often experienced when I was around the age of seventeen—an impatience, a let's-get-on-with-it kind of feeling. And I sense it again now. This transition sets in motion a great existential crisis—that is, a great captive urge. Part of this crisis is the sense that this is the point in life in which one's historical identity is solidified. Each of us leaves a mark on history, whether we deliberately choose to do so or not. And each of us has a direct responsibility for our legacy. When we reach fifty, this fact becomes clearer. We begin to reevaluate our lives, seek justifications. We ask hard questions: Are we satisfied with the contribution we have made so far? Are we taking advantage of the lessons we have learned? Are we aware of the ways in which our presence on earth has value?

We are often tempted to denigrate our worth as we grow

older, to say that our lives have not made that much difference. We are hard-pressed to name the grand achievements of our lives (beyond having children). And yet if we look, we will see that we have often defined human worth in rigid and superficial ways or hinged it on grandiose achievements. It is our task now to look beyond all of these and find the true measure of our personal worth. It *is* there.

I have sometimes used an exercise in psychotherapy groups that helps people face the question of their value head-on. I will ask those in the group to imagine that they are crowded together in a lifeboat, with no food or water. There are too many people in the boat, and the water is starting to spill over the top. "Unless one person goes overboard, everyone on the lifeboat will sink," I tell them. "Each of you has two minutes to make a case to the others for your being chosen to live."

People always have a very hard time with this exercise, especially groups of women, where there is a tendency to try to please others and make sacrifices. ("It's okay . . . I'll go overboard.") But even those who normally have high self-esteem find the exercise challenging. Few of us have ever put into words what we consider our value to be.

One of the most common barriers to self-esteem is the belief that there is a set period for achieving, that curiosity and risk belong only to the young. Once we reach fifty, the myth goes, it is time to tally up our achievements. And we are then sentenced to live out our remaining years, either in pride or in regret. What a grim and utterly false portrait this is!

For the most part the women I met while writing this book refused to sit still for these negative and demeaning conclusions. Their lives were filled with energy and growth; they were engaged in the world and busy making plans for the future. On several occasions I met women who had taken specific action to jolt themselves out of any suggestion of complacency. These women are worthy of note simply because they were able to demonstrate in such bold ways that the journey of life exists from birth to death, not from birth to middle age, and that the journey can take us wherever we want to go.

A Celebration of Fifty

I loved meeting Sally, a fifty-one-year-old housewife from the Midwest who had always dreamed of learning to skydive. It was a dream she rarely shared with others; in truth Sally had never been a particularly adventurous or physically active person, so she expected her desire to perform this dangerous feat to be hard for people to understand. Sally especially avoided telling her husband—even when the dream turned into a specific plan. She didn't want to argue about it. She didn't want to be lectured on the high risk. She just wanted to do it.

The opportunity presented itself while she was visiting her parents in Florida. Using the cover that she was going to see an old friend, she drove to a training school and took lessons.

Since Sally had waited so long for this opportunity, she wanted it to be perfect. She arranged for a videotape to be made of her jump, and she purchased a bright purple jumpsuit to wear. It was her choice to jump in tandem with another woman rather than solo. She was truly taking her life in her own hands—before the jump she had to sign a form freeing the company of any liability.

"We went up in a Cessna 52, and I was aware of everything," Sally recalled. "The buzzing of the plane, the yellow tops of the palm trees, the beating of my heart. When we reached ten thousand feet, it was time to jump, and it happened very fast. The man with the video camera jumped first so he could take pictures of us from the air. Then my partner and I—we were tethered together at the shoulders and hips—crossed our hands over our chests and stepped out of the plane at exactly the same instant.

"Actually it would be more accurate to say that we *flew* out of the plane, and I was surprised that we were head down at first. We free-fell for four thousand feet, then opened the parachutes and floated for six thousand feet. I wanted it to last forever. I have never felt so serene and in such control. It was magnificent.

"We landed right on target in an eighteen-foot-diameter sand pit, cared for by an eighty-three-year-old man who raked it daily and performed other chores in exchange for a weekly jump. As he told me, 'It's not age that's important—it's your frame of mind.'

"I took the film home and played it for my husband and children as proof of what I had done. Watching the amazement on their faces was almost as satisfying as making the jump."

Hearing Sally's story made me think of an expression I heard a lot when I was young but never hear now that I am older: "Can you take a dare?" Sally's inner voice had posed the dare, and she had taken it. Her family was shocked, not only because Sally had jumped out of a plane but because Sally had *wanted* to jump out of a plane. They were baffled by the impulse that drove her. Who would ever say to a fifty-one-year-old woman, "I dare you to jump out of a plane"?

A second meaningful encounter with a daring expression in middle life was with Penny, forty-nine, a vivacious, personable Florida travel agent. Penny described her most meaningful journey, the trip she took alone by car across the country.

"I wasn't running away," she said. "I was happily married and relatively content with my life. But as I moved into my late forties, I felt instinctively that I needed to break the mold, to reidentify myself as an individual in my own right. Deciding to go on a trip by myself was also a break with the past. It was the first time in my life I would be completely on my own, not taking care of others or having them take care of me."

Penny's husband had a difficult time understanding her decision to go off on her own. He felt threatened, as though he might be losing her. She did her best to calm his fears and solicit his support, and she was largely successful. Her trip, which lasted nearly three months, was taken in the bravest possible way, traveling along back roads instead of interstate highways, avoiding familiar restaurant and hotel chains in favor of havens that carried the flavor of the locale. Once she even slept alone outdoors at a campsite, something she had never done before.

Listening to Penny talk about her trip, it seemed that her day-to-day experiences became metaphors for the larger issues in her life. When she spoke of traveling at her own pace and feeling free to make frequent stops, she was reflecting about how harried her life had always been, how focused on the needs of others. "For the first time I was listening to my own inner voice and going where it wanted to take me," Penny said.

Two years after the fact Penny is still sorting out the full significance of the journey that launched her on a new phase of her life. But she knows that the trip accomplished one very important objective. "I learned to identify and pay attention to my own needs. It made me a more balanced individual. It's impossible to take a journey like mine and not gain a certain perspective about what's important in life," she said reflectively. "And now I know I can do anything I set out to do."

I use Sally and Penny as examples because their choices of personal expression are so vivid and rich in symbolism for all of us. But each individual must reach into her own life to find her unique statement of creativity. Often, as Sally and Penny have demonstrated, that means allowing another side of one's personality to emerge.

But since our expressions of creativity and daring do not exist in a vacuum, it is relevant to ask what they are in support of or what grander role, if any, they are preparing us to play. Recent studies on the dynamics of the middle years offer some very bright conclusions. One survey of twelve hundred middle-aged men and women, conducted by New World Decisions in Princeton, New Jersey, found that this period was most commonly marked by intense engagement, more direct contributions to community, and acts of altruism and caring—rather than by crisis, fear, and self-improvement. The study concluded that those people who did not find a way to make a contribution to the future in some way were left in a state of psychological stagnation and were more inclined to give in to the negative manifestations of aging.

Dr. Robert Michels, chairman of the psychiatry department at the Cornell Medical School, who has studied behavior patterns of middle-aged people, notes that people in their middle years begin to face the central crisis of later life, the approach of death. This, he suggests, is a positive thing, for the outcome is a new view of one's life and a consideration of the legacy one will leave for the future. It makes sense that middle-aged people would be more community-oriented and altruistic, says Dr. Michels, observing that "You gain a kind of symbolic immortality by furthering a group you belong to or a cause you identify with."

My husband, Bob, and I experienced this vividly last year when we decided to change the nature of our family Christmas celebration. Christmas had always been a special holiday for me, I think because it was so closely linked to the happy memories I had from the time when my children were young. But I'd noticed that in the last few years, as my children grew older and more independent, the holidays were looking less and less like the treasured old celebration. There were fewer (if any) breathless moments. People were always on the run; we attended church services at different times rather than as a family.

But it wasn't just that I was missing the old flavor of the holiday. I found, too, that I was feeling generally more reflective, my thoughts dwelling on the spirit of Christmas. I think one reason was that Bob, a devout Catholic, was not so enthusiastic about the secular manifestations of the celebration. But there was also the general inclination I was experiencing those days to reevaluate my basic assumptions and consider my life from a different perspective.

One morning in late autumn, as I sat drinking coffee in my spacious, bright kitchen, thinking about the upcoming holidays, I was overwhelmed by how much we had to be grateful for. It seemed that we had an abundance of blessings, almost more than our share. I also realized that one reason our Christmas celebrations had grown so dull was that they did not meet our needs, either physically or spiritually. I wondered what it would be like if this Christmas we threw aside the old customs and reached outside our immediate family. I remembered what the woman at the shelter for the homeless had said about the older women who found themselves suddenly outside the circle of love and support. Everything I knew from my Christian heritage and my human understanding made me see these homeless women as members of my community for whom I was responsible. Like many people, I had tried to do my share, but the problems of poverty and homelessness were too overwhelming. Nevertheless I decided that this Christmas we would make the homeless a part of our family celebration. Bob was equally enthusiastic about the idea, so I began to make calls, figuring it would be easy to find a location where we could help serve a meal on Christmas Day. But it was harder than I had expected. I made at least thirty calls before I found a place where we could volunteer. The organization was called Sharing Community, and it arranged for homeless people to be fed on Christmas Day at a Catholic church in Yonkers, New York.

The plans took firm shape in my mind before I told the children. We would, I decided, spend a few hours serving meals to the homeless and then return home for our own celebration. I would cook a large pot of stew, and we would eat, play carols, exchange gifts, and reflect about our experience. I expected the children to be very pleased with this plan. Surely they were equally aware of how pedestrian our celebrations had become in recent years—almost as though we were dragging ourselves through the rituals because it was expected. But I underestimated how important our traditional Christmas celebration had become for the children. They were not very happy about making a change.

Finally only my daughter, Kim, and Bob's daughter, Linda, joined us at the church. The others agreed to meet us back at the house afterward. On Christmas Day we attended an early Mass, then drove to Yonkers, arriving at the church at about ten o'clock in the morning. There was festive chaos when we arrived. The organizers assigned us to various tasks. The girls and I were assigned to help prepare and serve food. Bob was asked to remain outside in the parking lot to direct the homeless people inside.

Soon after we arrived, I looked up to find the large hall already filling with people of all ages. I was particularly struck by how many children there were and how many elderly.

Somewhere along the way, in the process of heaping turkey

and potatoes and cranberry sauce and pie onto their plates, the homeless people who filled the room ceased being the objects of my charity (my good deed) and became participants in a common celebration, every bit as special to me in that moment and in that room as the members of my family had been sitting around our Christmas tree for all those years. And as that dawned on me, I saw that it was not enough to fill their plates with food—a grim duty. I wanted to give them the celebration as well.

One of the priests was feeling the same way. "What would really answer my prayers right now would be if we had someone to play the piano," he said, looking wistfully out over the crowded tables of people.

"My husband, Bob, plays the piano," I said, feeling incredibly happy to be able to share this piece of good news. "He's outside showing people in."

"Do you think he could play some Christmas music?"

"Yes, I'm sure he would." I ran out to get Bob, who was happy to oblige. He sat down at the piano and began to play by ear . . .

Hark the herald angels sing
Glory to the newborn King . . .

And suddenly it was Christmas. The piano was old, in desperate need of tuning, and the notes struggled to fill the room above the clamor, but gradually the familiar music struck a common chord of response. I noticed that many people were swaying and singing along.

It's easy for us to forget—or never to realize in the first place—the basic things we have in common with others, even when we live very different lives. The music created a common surge of sentiment in the room. And as I began to move among the people and talk to them, I saw how I, like most people, had found it so much easier and more convenient to wall myself off emotionally from the homeless (and, indeed, from so many others who were different from me). Now I was meeting them, learning their names, talking to their children, enjoying myself in their presence.

It is that kind of experience that changes people, and as we drove home late that afternoon, laughing and talking, eager to recount moments from the day, I knew that in some small but absolute way we would all think very differently in the future about what it meant for us to be family and part of the human community.

※ ※

Our new expressions of creativity and caring enable us to absolve ourselves of regret for the things we did not do in the past. They rescue us from living in despair over our regrets. For it is only human to have regrets, and as we grow older we often find that we walk with one eye cocked over our shoulder, wishing for what might have been.

Every person alive has regrets. When Nadine Stair, of Louisville, Kentucky, wrote the following words, she was eighty-five years old:

> If I had my life to live over, I'd care to make more mistakes next time. I would limber up. I would be sillier than I have been this trip. I would take fewer things seriously. I would take more chances. I would climb more mountains and swim more rivers. I would perhaps have more actual troubles, but I'd have fewer imaginary ones.
>
> You see, I'm one of those people who lives sensibly and sanely, hour after hour, day after day. Oh, I've had my moments, and if I had to do it over again, I'd have more of them. In fact, I'd try to have nothing else. Just moments, one after another, instead of living so many years ahead of each day.
>
> I've been one of those persons who never goes anywhere without a thermometer, a hot water bottle, a raincoat, and a parachute. If I had to do it again, I would travel lighter than I have.
>
> If I had my life to live over, I would start barefoot earlier in the spring and stay that way later in the fall. I

would go to more dances. I would ride more merry-go-rounds. I would pick more daisies.

When I first read this, I identified completely with these sentiments, even though I was much younger than the author. Once youth is past, we often begin this process of identifying our regrets and visualizing the ways we could have made our lives different if only we could be given another chance.

But what happens when our regrets about the past collide with our dreams and the possibilities of our futures? As Ernest A. Fitzgerald, a bishop of the United Methodist Church, wrote, "The middle years need not be years of lost dreams. Indeed, these years can be the most productive of all. A study of the biographies of great people reveals that those who have made the greatest contributions have made them not while they were young but when they were older." So, even as we envy the young their opportunities, our own greatest promise may still lie before us. Instinctively we recognize that it is time now to start naming our lives, and we can choose words of acceptance or words of regret. It is this choice that determines who we will be in the years ahead.

※ ※

For the past three years my old school friend Diane and six other women in Malibu, a beach community near Los Angeles, have met once a month in a very different kind of gathering from those I had observed elsewhere. As Diane had explained it when she invited me to attend one of their meetings, the group used a format called the Council Method, which was adapted from a Native American tradition. What made the approach especially interesting to me was its reliance on ritual to help the women articulate and affirm their feelings and ideas.

The women in the group ranged in age from their late forties to early sixties, and for this reason, Diane told me, the topics raised were often related to the transition points of their lives. "When we started the group, we began looking for wise elders—women who would be our role models for aging. But we couldn't find any, so we decided that we would be our own role models."

Each month, Diane explained, the group's leader, a woman in her forties named Sue, would choose a topic. This day, because of my presence, the topic would be about growing older. As the women gathered in the center of Diane's spacious living room, conversation stopped and there was an atmosphere of reverence. I felt honored to be included.

We stood in a circle, holding hands. Sue spoke quietly, acknowledging the presence of each person and mentioning by name those who were unable to be present. She asked us to look directly into each other's eyes as a way of acknowledging our connection, and I found it to be a powerful moment. It is not often that people stop and look one another straight in the eye—our glances more often slide off the center and just miss being intimate. After a few moments Sue spoke again, asking each person in the group to get in touch with her feelings about growing older. When she finished speaking, we sat in the chairs and couches that were arranged behind us in a circle. Sue pulled out a large, gnarled piece of driftwood, about two feet long. It shone, smooth and polished; beaded ribbons attached to the wood rattled as she passed it around the circle. This wonderful "talking stick" seemed almost magical; indeed it functioned as an agent of reflection. Each women held the stick as she spoke and passed it to her neighbor when she finished.

As each person took her turn holding the stick and speaking about her feelings, I was impressed by how closely the sentiments of these women echoed those I had been hearing in my travels across the country. I reflected that women of our generation really do have a shared experience, in spite of the diversity of our heritages. When it was my turn to speak, I reminded them of that fact, and emphasized my deep belief that the tremendous power we possess as women comes from this shared energy.

Sue had brought poems that she asked us to read aloud. They were about different aspects of women growing older.

We started around the circle, each reading the poem we had been given. Words and lines made us laugh and nod knowingly. Diane read a poem by Leah Schweitzer, called "Self Adjustments," that brought a smile of recognition to every face:

> ... this morning I noticed
> a new, blue vein
> barely visible
> yet unmistakably there
> tattooed to my left breast,
> a tree branch, twisting,
> reaching, stretching
> out to the nipple, and
> I didn't much care
> for the way it offended
> my sense of the aesthetic ...

Barbara, a divorced woman of forty-eight, read a poem of her own, called "Ojai Dance." It was rich with Native American symbolism and was inspirational:

> Out from behind their masks
> they've come
> the frightened
> the timid
> the cynical ones
> Masks worn for protection
> Masks creating isolation
>
> Out from behind our masks
> we've come
> Opening our minds
> our eyes
> our hearts
> Daring to be open each moment
> Daring to change, to rearrange
>
> At last—secure in the knowing
> We are loved!
> Whether in our make-up
> or without our masquerade
> We are loved!

No matter what!
Ho!

After other poems were read, including Diane's "Baggy-wrinkle" (reprinted on page xi), which made all of us laugh through teary eyes, Sue introduced a poem she had written herself. Titled "That Old Woman," it reflected her mixed feelings about aging.

> Tonight my sadness overwhelms me
> I wallow in it as pigs in mud mid August
> The same discomfort belongs to us both
> They cannot sweat and I cannot weep
> Externally everything looks fine
> I am an attractive woman
> Who does not wear her forty years
> for all to see.
> But, oh, how the years
> have turned me gray and wrinkled
> and a bit stooped over on the inside
> I long to be held and loved,
> to feel sixteen again
> Instead I lie here alone amid the flowered sheets
> Except for the company of that old woman.

I read a poem written by Ruth Harriet Jacobs, a psychologist and poet affiliated with the Wellesley College Center for Research on Women. Harriet sent it to me to use here. It is a beautiful piece, titled "At Sixty-Three."

> What I want for the rest of my life
> is to live simply and joyfully
> close to nature and God
> ministering, as I am led to do
> to people in new ways,
> communicating with my children
> as equals without dependency
> or guilt on either side
> or the reliving of old history.
>
> What I want for the rest of my life
> is to accept that in my living

I made some serious mistakes
but did the best I could at the time.
I want to stop blaming myself
and have as much compassion and respect
for myself as I have for others.

I want to travel to new places
to witness and be touched
by the stories of others
then tell their stories
in my books and poetry
to help people see themselves
in others and know we are all
kindred spirits within the spirit,
and that what injures one of us
insults all of us
while the triumph of one of us
is a mountain climbed by all.

What I want for the rest of my life
is to deal gracefully and graciously
with the decrements of aging
so that by example and testimony
I give others the courage
to see that the missions and ministry
of the aged are as important as of youth
and are important to youth.

Finally, I want to meet my death knowing
that I lived fully, returning to life
the talents and time given me by grace.

After the readings Sue looked around the circle and asked if anyone had something to add. We talked about the feelings the poems evoked in us, touching on many of the themes we have explored so far in this book. I noticed that even though sometimes the poems were sad, our experience of having read them together was cathartic.

When we had finished talking about the poetry, Sue motioned us to stand again and hold hands. I could feel the electricity that moved into me from the women on each side. We stood that way for a moment, our eyes bright with the experience. Sue spoke of the special connection of feelings present in the group and reiterated the pledge the group had made to care for one another. Then the session, which had taken about an hour and a half, was over. We dropped hands, and everyone stood in place for a moment, making the mental transition back to the world.

"As a society we have set aside much of the ritual in our lives or rendered it mundane," Sue said to me later. "Now I think that people are slowly beginning to come back to it. Look at the way these old Indian rituals speak to us."

"And it isn't just that we are borrowing the ritual," added Diane. "We are creating a new ritual that may become something important for future generations of women."

I was deeply affected by my afternoon's experience, and after the Malibu visit I began to do further reading about the role of rituals in human development and interaction. Echoing my feelings about our family Christmas celebration, a psychotherapist who uses ritual in her practice said, "Many of our culture's sacred ceremonies have become empty rituals. They no longer heal imbalances or celebrate passages in the human journey. The result is a culture that suffers from what the primal mind would call loss of soul."

It may be this sense of loss that has driven so many people back to organized religion. But the rituals of traditional religion, which have been dominated by male imagery, do not always speak to women. This may be the reason that women have been at the forefront of study and experiment with new rituals. Indeed neither our religious nor our secular traditions have included formal ways to celebrate the most significant passages that occur in women's lives. This was certainly made clear to me as I listened to so many women struggle with a way to mark, and to celebrate, turning fifty.

❈ ❈

As I completed this book, the writing of which has been a remarkable journey for me, as I hope its reading will be for you, my fiftieth birthday approached—due to occur shortly before the book's publication date. In one respect I recognized that the celebration of my fiftieth birthday would be a very public matter because it would coincide with the book's publication and promotion. But even as I completed the book, the script for my personal celebration remained unfinished.

The turning-fifty birthday ritual was the prevailing image I carried with me as I wrote this book. The title was chosen carefully because I wanted to communicate my belief that celebration is appropriate for this life passage. But not celebration in the frivolous, ungenuine, rah-rah way it is so often expressed. And certainly not the greeting card industry's idea of celebrating fifty, which would have us burning our birth certificates in bonfires.

I believe we have to reach down deep to shape a definition for this kind of celebration. And as I considered the past fifty years of my own life, I grappled for the best way to acknowledge the past and point myself to the future.

I finally decided that my birthday celebration would bring together these joint themes of dreams and regrets. Specifically it would be about letting go of my regrets—really giving them up—so my life would be free and clear to allow me to explore the potential of the coming years. And so, months before the fact, I created a plan for my celebration of fifty.

In the months and weeks before my birthday, I will consider my life—who I have been, the roles I have played, how I have lived, what I have achieved and failed to achieve. And I will write down on individual cards my regrets from fifty years of life. The purpose will not be to beat myself up, as so many women our age do, but to validate and affirm my life by acknowledging and then letting go of my sadnesses about the past.

On the day of my birthday we will have a lovely dinner, just Bob, Scott, Kim, and me. They will prepare it, of course. The centerpiece on our dinner table will be a colorful bunch of helium balloons—red, blue, silver, yellow—about ten of them. And after we finish eating, I will read each of my regret cards out loud—and maybe comment on it or ask Bob or the kids to comment; I'm not sure about that part yet. And then we will attach each card to a balloon. After this is done, we will rise from the table, each of us carrying some of the balloons. Together we will take them outside, down the steps of the back porch to the grass. Standing in the center of the yard, we will let go of the balloons, and they will sail up above the trees.

I have a picture of it in my mind. We are standing, the four of us, in a circle on the grass, and our heads are thrown way back, because we are all looking up. We remain that way until we can no longer see a single balloon, until they all have disappeared to float toward the mountains or the towering buildings of Manhattan, then out to sea. And once they are gone, I will be free to pursue the coming years without their burden. Remaining then will be only the dreams that determine what contribution I make in the next phase of my life.

WRITING YOUR BIRTHDAY RITUAL

The most important piece of advice I have for women who are contemplating their fiftieth birthday is to be sure to celebrate it. Mark it as an important birthday. Don't let it go or sweep it under the rug. I've found that women who make a point of ritualizing this turning point get so much out of it. Often the act of celebrating fifty turns around women who previously had felt fearful or depressed about reaching this age.

A good way to ritualize the turning point that fifty represents is to think of this birthday as being the demarcation point between the past and the future. The joint themes of letting go of regrets and fulfilling your dreams in the future can be very movingly symbolized. Knowing that you are not trapped by the past can make you feel strong and give you a new sense of anticipation about the future.

The birthday ritual should be very personal, so you should ask yourself what it would mean for you to bring together the past and the future in a celebratory way. Here are a few ideas other women have suggested. You may find that one of them touches you in particular.

"I arranged a luncheon with the three generations of

women in my family—my mother, my sister, and my daughter. At the luncheon I gave each of them a gift to symbolize the role they played in my life. And we talked about all the things we shared as women. It was the first time we had ever talked like that, and all of us were very moved."

"I had a party just for my women friends. There was a cake and champagne. In advance I asked each woman to think of a toast she could give to our future. I tape-recorded the toast-giving and sent everyone copies of the tape."

"My best friend planned a party. Instead of the usual gifts, she asked each person to bring the one thing that I could take with me on my journey into the future. When they presented their gifts, they said what they intended the gift to mean for me. The gifts included everything from a book of poetry to serve as inspiration to a silk negligee to remind me how sexy I still am."

"I called up two friends of the same age I had not seen in many years, who lived in different parts of the country, and arranged a reunion. Reconnecting with these old friends was the best way I could possibly celebrate!"

"I made my own birthday card and sent it to everyone I knew—all the people on my Christmas list. The front of the card read, 'Good News! Marian's 50.' Inside I wrote a little poem about being given the gift of a healthy life and good friends."

In whatever way you choose to celebrate your fiftieth birthday, make it a time when you stop to appreciate yourself. Think of how many lives you've touched in your fifty years, how many contributions, great and small, you've made to others. And make a promise to yourself that during the coming years you will not lose sight of how rare and valuable your presence in the world is.

Appendix A
Recommended Reading

Adams, Alice. *Second Chances.* New York: Alfred A. Knopf, 1988.

Atoniak, Helen, et al. *Alone: Emotional, Legal and Financial Help for the Widowed or Divorced Woman.* Milbrae, CA: Les Femmes/Celestial Arts, 1979.

Atwood, Margaret. *Cat's Eye.* New York: Doubleday, 1989.

Bassoff, Evelyn, Ph.D. *Mothers and Daughters.* New York: New American Library, 1989.

Bennett, Helen. "Two of Us Is One Too Many." *New York Times Magazine,* October 22, 1989.

Bernikow, Louise. *Alone in America: The Search for Companionship.* New York: Harper & Row, 1986.

Bloomfield, Harold. *Making Peace with Your Parents.* New York: Random House, 1983.

Bowe, Claudia. "The UP Generation. The Lear's Report on How Women Feel." *Lear's,* March 1989.

Caine, Lynn. *Lifelines.* New York: Doubleday, 1978.

Caine, Lynn. *Widow.* New York: Bantam, 1981.

Cole, K. C. "Aging Bull." *Ms.*, April 1989.

Corman, Avery. *50.* New York: Simon & Schuster, 1987.

Cutler, Winnifred B., Ph.D. *Hysterectomy—Before and After.* New York: Harper & Row, 1988.

DeCrow, Karen. "The Significance of Becoming 50." *New York Times*, January 7, 1988.

Doress, Paula Brown; Siegal, Diane Laskin; and The Middle and Older Women's Book Project; in cooperation with the Boston Women's Health Book Collective. *Ourselves Growing Older.* New York: Simon & Schuster, 1987.

Dychtwald, Ken, Ph.D, and Flower, Joe. *Age Wave: The Challenges and Opportunities of an Aging America.* Los Angeles: Jeremy P. Tarcher, Inc., 1989.

Fonda, Jane. *Women Coming of Age.* New York: Simon & Schuster, 1984.

Freedman, Rita, Ph.D. *Bodylove: Learning to Like Our Looks—and Ourselves.* New York: Harper & Row, 1988.

Goleman, Daniel. "For Many, Turmoil of Aging Erupts in the 50's, Studies Find." *New York Times*, February 7, 1989.

Hale, Christine. "A New Wrinkle on Aging." *Women's News*, July 1988.

Heilbrun, Carolyn B. *Writing a Woman's Life.* New York: W. W. Norton & Company, 1988.

Kollata, Gina. "Cancer Fears Throw Spotlight on Estrogen." *New York Times*, January 17, 1989.

Koller, Alice. *An Unknown Woman.* New York: Bantam Books, 1981.

Kornhaber, Arthur, and Woodward, Kenneth L. *Grandparents/Grandchildren: The Vital Connection.* New York: Doubleday, 1981.

Appendix A: Recommended Reading

Krementz, Jill. *How It Feels When a Parent Dies.* New York: Alfred A. Knopf, 1981.

Kupfer, Fran. *Surviving the Seasons.* New York: Dell Publishing, 1987.

Kutner, Lawrence. "When Young Adults Head Back Home." *New York Times,* July 14, 1988.

Ladas, Alice K., Ed.D. "Sex and Intimacy in the Second Half of Life." *Women's News,* July 1988.

Lear, Frances. "Redefining Beauty." *Lear's,* October 1989.

Leslie, Connie. "The Graying of the Campus." *Newsweek,* June 6, 1988.

Loewinsohn, Ruth J. *Survival Handbook for Widows.* Chicago: Follett, 1979.

Maitland, Margaret Todd. "Milestones." *Minneapolis/St. Paul,* November 1988.

McConnell, Adeline, and Anderson, Beverly. *Single After Fifty.* New York: McGraw-Hill, 1980.

Morganroth Gullette, Margaret. "Midlife Exhilaration." *New York Times Magazine,* January 29, 1989.

Morganroth Gullette, Margaret. *Safe at Last in the Middle Years.* Los Angeles: University of California Press, 1988.

Olds, Sally Wendkos. *The Eternal Garden—Seasons of Our Sexuality.* New York: Times Books, 1985.

Pogrebin, Letty Cottin. *Among Friends.* New York: McGraw Hill, 1987.

Shreve, Anita. *Women Together, Women Alone.* New York: Viking/Penguin, 1989.

Smiley, Jane. *Ordinary Love & Good Will.* New York: Alfred A. Knopf, 1989.

Stein, Charlotte Markman. "Age of Enlightenment." *Ms.,* August 1988.

Sullivan, Tobie. "No Regrets." *New Woman,* March 1988.

Tyler, Anne. *Breathing Lessons*, New York: Alfred A. Knopf, 1988.

Viorst, Judith. *Forever Fifty and Other Negotiations*. New York: Simon & Schuster, 1989.

Viorst, Judith. *Necessary Losses*. New York: Ballantine Books, 1986.

Voda, Ann M., R.N., Ph.D., and Eliasson, Mona, Ph.D. *Menopause: The Closure of Menstrual Life*. New York: Haworth Press, 1983.

Voda, Ann M., R.N., Ph.D., with Tucker, James. *Menopause and You*. Salt Lake City: University of Utah College of Nursing, 1984.

Wells, Linda. "As Times Goes By." *New York Times Magazine*, March 19, 1989.

Appendix B
Reader Survey: Turning Fifty

As part of a continuing study of the psychology of women growing older, I would be interested in hearing from more women on this topic. If you are willing to participate in this study, please fill out the following questionnaire and return it to me at the address listed below. Thank you for your support.

1. Age _____

2. Race/Ethnic Background _____

3. Marital Status: ____ Married ____ Separated
   ____ Widowed ____ Divorced ____ Single

4. Religion _____

5. Family Income: ____ Over $50,000
   ____ $25,000-50,000 ____ $15,000-25,000
   ____ Less than $15,000

6. Children: ____ Number _____ Ages

7. Mark with an X where you think you are now on your birth-to-death life line:
BIRTH _____ DEATH

8. To what age do you think you will live?____

9. How old do you feel now?____

(Check all that apply for the following questions.)

10. How did you celebrate (or plan to celebrate) your fiftieth birthday?
    ____ The way I usually celebrate birthdays
    ____ In a special way
    ____ Not at all

11. What surprises you about the experiences of turning fifty?
    ____ I feel so much younger than I thought I would feel at this age.
    ____ I look so much younger than I anticipated I would feel at fifty.
    ____ Other people respond to me differently than they used to.
    ____ I'm not sad about it.
    ____ I'm so different than my mother was at this age.
    ____ I'm not surprised—it's what I expected.
    ____ Other (please elaborate):

12. Looking back, what are your regrets about the past—and what would you have done differently?
    ____ I would have chosen a different career.
    ____ I would have had children (more children).
    ____ I would have waited longer to marry.

Appendix B: Reader Survey: Turning Fifty

____ I would have cultivated more friendships.
____ I would have traveled more.
____ I would have pursued higher education.
____ I would have taken better care of my health.
____ Other (please elaborate):

13. How do you feel about the future?
    ____ Optimistic and full of plans
    ____ Eager to make changes
    ____ Afraid of what will happen to me
    ____ Like I don't have much time
    ____ Other (please elaborate):

14. Rank in order of importance (1-10) where each of the following fits into your primary goals for the future:
    ____ Career   ____ Travel   ____ Relationships
    ____ Family   ____ Sexuality ____ Community
    ____ Health   ____ Money   ____ Education
    ____ Spirituality

15. In the past, work (paid or unpaid) has played:
    ____ a very important role in my life.
    ____ a somewhat important role in my life.
    ____ a less important role than other things.
    ____ an unimportant role in my life.

16. Have you ever lied about your age? ____ YES ____ NO
    (If YES, please explain)

17. What is your sex life like now, compared to a few years ago?
    ____ Better than ever

____ Less frequent, but more satisfying
____ Only satisfying some of the time
____ Full of problems that seem related to growing older
____ I have no current sex partner
____ Other (please elaborate):

18. What has been your physical experience of menopause?
____ I have not started menopause.
____ My menstrual periods are irregular (or have stopped), but there are no other symptoms.
____ I have occasional "hot flashes," but they're not serious.
____ I have severe "hot flashes."
____ I have many physical symptoms, including low energy and lack of sexual interest.
____ Other (please elaborate):

19. What has been your emotional experience of menopause?
____ There has been no emotional change.
____ I feel depressed and edgy.
____ I feel less attractive.
____ I'm afraid to have sex.
____ I'm embarrassed by "hot flashes."
____ I feel relieved to be past childbearing.
____ I feel freer.
____ Other (please elaborate):

20. How do you feel about your looks?
____ I look good and take care of myself.
____ I look okay but plan to have plastic surgery.

Appendix B: Reader Survey: Turning Fifty 171

_____ I'm worried that I look old.
_____ I'm resigned to looking older.
_____ I dress to look younger than I am.
_____ Other (please elaborate):

21. Who do you feel depends on you for day-to-day practical and emotional support?
_____ Husband _____ Parents _____ Others
_____ Children _____ Grandchildren

22. What would you need right now to really feel secure?
_____ Money _____ Marriage _____ Children nearby
_____ Property _____ A man _____ Health
_____ Career _____ Education _____ Religion
_____ Other (please elaborate):

23. If you have adult children, how do you feel about your relationship with them now?
_____ I'm comfortable with how close we are.
_____ I feel they sometimes take advantage of me.
_____ I'd like our relationship to be closer.
_____ I'm relieved they're finally on their own.
_____ I feel they're still too dependent on me.
_____ Other (please elaborate):

24. If you've never married, how do you feel about it now?
_____ I'm embarrassed to still be single.
_____ I'd like to be married, but I worry that it's too late.
_____ I enjoy being independent.
_____ Being married has never been a big priority in my life.

_____ I worry that it means there's something wrong with me.
_____ I regret never having children.
_____ I'm still planning to marry in the future.
_____ Other (please elaborate):

25. If you are married or have been married, what has been the importance of marriage in your life?
    _____ It's been the source of most of my satisfaction.
    _____ It's given me great satisfaction, along with other things—like career, children, religion, and friends.
    _____ I can't imagine not being married.
    _____ It's been the source of emotional pain.
    _____ There have been ups and downs, but it's been mostly positive.
    _____ Other (please elaborate):

26. What role do your women friends now play in your life?
    _____ We're closer than ever.
    _____ I've made close new friends.
    _____ I've remained close to old friends.
    _____ I no longer have patience for friends who take advantage of me.
    _____ I see myself growing old with my friends.
    _____ Other (please elaborate):

27. Other comments:

Appendix B: Reader Survey: Turning Fifty 173

(Optional)

NAME _____

ADDRESS _____

CITY _____ STATE _____ ZIP _____

TELEPHONE: (   ) _____

Please send your replies to: Karen Blaker, Ph.D.
                            611 Purchase Street
                            Rye, New York, 10580